# SIMUL

## Lutheran Voices in Poetry

*Edited by*

**MARK PATRICK ODLAND**

# CONTENTS

# PREFACE

While serving at a church in 2005 I began to dream about publishing an anthology of poetry written exclusively by Lutherans. When I shared this idea with others, responses ranged from "Oh, that's nice," to "What's Lutheran poetry?" Still others thought the project would fail. One famous Lutheran poet specifically emailed me saying, "I don't think this is a good idea. You'll just get a lot of bad poems with a faint Lutheran perfume on them."

Well, I am pleased to say that there is indeed a faint Lutheran perfume wafting through the air! However, I believe the poetry is superb, and I have been astounded at the depth of creative talent in the Lutheran church. After personally contacting 28 Lutheran colleges, 8 Lutheran seminaries, and almost 8,000 Lutheran congregations, the poetry submissions poured in by the hundreds.

When the final deadline had passed, I had received over 1,200 poems written by pastors, professors, and dozens of everyday Lutherans from all walks of life. Deciding which poetry to accept was very difficult, but I eventually narrowed it down to the poems I felt best fit the goals of the anthology. Selected authors range from newly discovered talent to well-known Lutheran poets and hymn writers. To hear their stories and read their poetry was a great gift to me, and I will be forever grateful for the experience.

It was my hope that this project would not only bring together the best poetry the Lutheran church has to offer, but encourage Lutherans around the country to deepen and discover their creative gifts as well. Because I only accepted submissions of previously unpublished poetry, many poets received the gentle nudge they needed to put pen to paper and write. As the project began, the question continued to linger in my mind, "What exactly is Lutheran poetry?"

I wondered, "Would denominational identity be enough to unify the book? What, if anything would make Lutheran voices in poetry different from any other group?" After wrestling with these kinds of questions, I determined that if there were to be a common thread that held the book together, it would have to be deeper than worship preferences or cultural traditions. In order to capture the complexity of our human existence and lives of faith, I chose to use the Lutheran theological understanding of the *SIMUL* as the book's guiding principle. To give the project clarity and direction, I included the following statement in my poetry guidelines:

"*SIMUL* is a publication of poetry that gladly accepts submissions from all those who identify themselves with the Lutheran faith tradition. The name of this anthology reflects Martin Luther's observation that as children of God we are both fully saints and fully sinners simultaneously. It is the goal of *SIMUL* to reflect this paradox, and explore the complexity, beauty, and messiness of the human condition. Poems submitted need not be 'religious,' but they must be honest. Laughter and tears, faith and doubt, hope and despair all have their place in this unique publication."

In response to this vision, there was an outpouring of creativity that surpassed all my wildest expectations! Indeed, a broad range of human emotion and experience have been captured within the poems of this book, and the authors have tackled heavy issues with great honesty and courage. It is my hope and prayer that these poems might find a place in your heart, and that they might be a blessing to you and your family now and for years to come.

In Christ,

Pastor Mark Odland, editor

*"For the wages of sin is death,*
*but the free gift of God is eternal life in Christ Jesus our Lord."*

*(Romans 6:23)*

# Jesus, Raptor

*Steve Swanson*

Jesus, raptor, now devour my rabbit spleen
Gorge yourself on every unseen fear
For I should rather die unbowelled
Than brook this bland timidity
Make me brave as you are brave, and were
Make me faithful, wise, and sure
Make us one as rain and cloud are one
For you and I together may not be
By cowardice or sloth undone
Your light must be proclaimed
Your truth, your way
Make me your spinal voice
Today

# Shape Is Determinant Of Meaning

*Kirby Olson*

Eggs are ovals

And cars flutter by on wings

Trash cans are cylindrical

Basketballs are spherical

Stars are pointy like star-fish

Nobody knows the eyes are stars

The world is outlined like a hockey rink

Lakes of green jello all over Minnesota

Lakes of pancake batter all over Lutheran church basements

The African savannah is peopled with giraffes

The sweet warm weather in her sweater

Everything that I know indicates

That the truth shall be known

A square shall become a triangle

# Life, Death & Resurrection

*Megan M. Rohrer*


do you see the new buds in my good soil
rising from my brokenness
turning old scars into new flesh
as they rise above…


do you see my lost childhood
the broken marrow in my bones
the demons attacked by holy water
the undulating silence of pain so deep


can you hear my voice
over the loud thoughts of your brain
calling you to reach beyond yourself
to the vulnerability of each new day

# Last In Line

*Kevin David Bergeson*

Think I found it
where the line ends:
clouded and curling
but here it's near.

Last in line
is the place to be:
giving away
what's mine, freely.
Paper trail
leads to the last in line.

When language is weak,
so is theology.
When I am full,
I need to let it go through my hands.

# truth murdered

*Rebecca F. Miller*

they would have me,
wrestling, wrangle my pale neck
beneath their multiple, shivering hands
violent and eager-blood
and leave me murdered in an alley,
stuffed in a dumpster, my eyes popping wide
from the moment the air left my throat
maybe they could kill me,
synthesizing cleverness: i dead and undead all at once
proclaim it in their polished courts
and lofty classrooms. and yet i would remain
slaughtered in a dumpster,
decaying on a heap of festering diapers
beside a hollowed television.  and the ghost of me
would creep behind their ears
before they closed their eyes at night
tickle and tingle a little unrest unaware
while they live and don't live all at once.

# The Daily Grind

*David M. Frye*

Each day she sits by the door
her bags gathered around her feet
like puppies
her quilted coat disguising her
invisibilizing her.
From the corner of my eye
as I load up my Venti half estate-grown half decaf Verona
double sweet a little cream
I watch her nurse a tall hot one.
Her hands cradle the sleeved cup
she inhales the steamed aroma coiling upwards
her eyes slitted, yet twinkling.

Each day this week I'd seen her gesture
as patrons entered by the side door
a gesture or a twitch, hard to tell.
Today I decide to give up
stop pretending I didn't see her.
I toss the wooden stir stick
and the spent brown sugar packets
into the trash
and turn around.

I smile at her and say good morning
she smiles back
her lips' wrinkled corners rising
lifts her right hand
it moves like always.
A twitch? No.
The sign of the cross. Amen.

# Clear And Perfect

*Katherine Kennon*

I know it's dark, but try to see.
The time it takes won't be in vain.
Just open wide and feel the light
Behind and underneath the pain.
It's somewhere that the throne of life
Cannot accommodate in space,
Where nonetheless, it stretches out
To lay a groundwork built on grace.
Afraid of death, we move toward life,
Though many ships have sailed and sank.
Afraid of going under here,
And questioning the one we thank.
Afraid of death, we move aside
Into a shadow overused,
But in the light, there are no corners,
Just a clear and perfect view.
I know it's faint, but try to hear
The whispering of endless dreams.
Just open wide and feel the beating
Current of the one esteem.
It's somewhere that a million tears
Could never overcast a garnet.
Where wind and ice may taunt the sun,
But in the end could never harm it.
I know you're doubting in the dark,
And one man's question may deny,
But open wide the arms you have,
And let the universe inside.
Somewhere waits a blinding star
That means to give you better sights,
Replacing hours with eternity-
Heavy hearts to endless flights.
I know it's dark, but in the light
You'll find forever points the way-
A gesture of the weathered sunshine
With some clear and perfect rays.

# Fully God and Fully Human

*Le Anne Clausen*

Jesus,
Whatever else beyond our comprehension he was,
Was born into the world an earthly being
The same way all the rest of us earthly beings were:
Between a woman's legs,
With all the blood and feces and amniosis

And with all the screaming
And gasping for air
That birth entails.

For all his other human experiences
And his violent suffering bleeding death,
Why do we insist
On an inhumanly calm and sanitized
Nativity?

# SONNET

*Caleb Hendrickson*

*Complacency* need not ring odious
In ear or soul as do *sloth* unpleasant
And *languor* vile, such words are scandalous
To a calm heart whose beat is confident.
Though April may be cruel and torrential
Let us make May our model, for it brings
Quiet verdure, April's storms forgotten all,
And comes to passing on complacent wings.
Knowing we're liked, relaxing into that
Which spoilt death, the sheep gate two ways swinging,
That we might be May blooms, fed with the dirt
To which we are eagerly returning,
Serenely sipping of the sun's favor
That we an endless spring have to savor.

# VULTURES

*Mary Koeberl*

Circling, searching, soaring.
Blackened eagles sweeping the sky, with giant wings.
Standing, guarding, huddling.
Sorrowful mourners around an open grave.
Beautiful creatures,
Scorned by man,
Waiting on death for life.
Playing their special part in nature's perfect plan.

# In The Grand Scale Of Things

*Frank Attanasia*

In the grand scale of things
My thoughts are tiny paper boats
Fierce feisty wind makes them capsize
Some disappear, sinking quickly
Others resurface not looking the same
Resolute, they journey onward
Voices cry, "captain, to what port are
they headed?"
Alas, one would think I should know
But looks deceive, I am only a deckhand
In the grand scale of things

# HOPE

*Christine Jensen*

Scattered, ripped couch cushions
lifted from dusty squares,
empty coat pockets lined
with panicked, hungry hands.
Stained, white shelves in a
condiment occupied fridge,
a last resort from vacant shelves of
rice and pasta hairs.

A cigarette butt, cool in the tray,
an addict's final treasure,
creates a void from tension sweat,
from contact with his pleasure.
If words were dollars, time copper pennies
and addiction a debt paid,
cushions would be straight, pockets filled,
and souls once more unafraid.

# in the vein

*Ned Hayes*

your absence hisses
  in my mouth
a stone on the lips.

  you've seeped out of me, an intoxication
of memory, bitter as the peel of an orange,
sharp as a curl of cinnamon skin,
  I know it like a poison
in the vein

  it moves through me, this
missing of you, a slow shudder
  something distant and
unknowable comes close,
  underground, where I post no sentries,
keep no code-breakers,
  where I am blind.

  in the morning you
have moved darker through
  me, and I know all
that I can bring into this room
  is not enough
to fill it.

# Compassion Innate

*Helen Eikamp*

The manchild clutches soldier gear
and stalks with fear
through haze of dawn
to happen on
a manchild of the enemy,
and suddenly
they pause, hearts leap,
two souls reach deep
beyond dark webs of savage hate
to question fate
with eyes that see
shared empathy.

# Tree Bonking

*Ann Dixon*

When stout birches bow
beneath loads of snow
like supplicants, by grief
bent low, I cannot help
but sympathize.
One inch of snow, a sudden
freeze and some will snap —
become dead trees.

Can I halt immoral wars?
Save savaged children?
One oil-slicked shore?
Perhaps. Or not.
But I can be the rescuer
of many trees.

It isn't much, to free a tree
compared to helping
humanity. Nonetheless,
I shake and poke
till snow descends in heaps
of hope, releasing branches
that reach and rise eagerly
toward bluest sky.

# Last Days at Holden Village, 1996

*Flo Pendergrast*

Waiting for the moon,
my volunteer days are ending
and I am glad, I am tired,
tired of laundry and back aches….
But this evening,
surrounded by low talk and laughter,
I sit by the blonde, sunny Sarah, from Bellevue,
sitting in the "Ark" .. waiting for the full moon.
We talk of great moons we have seen;
how the moon rising over Eagle lake
shed beams that danced
in a shimmering line across the water.
How, when you cross the I-90 bridge
into Seattle, the full moon
is an orange fantasma upon the waters.
How the autumn moon rising
over the horizon in Colorado
is so huge and orange,
full, unbelievably grand.
But, now tonight we wait in vain,
the full moon is hiding
behind the tall peaks
and bedtime calls.

# The Feast

*Chuck Huff*

There must have been extra wheat flour that day
for young and old, with and without teeth,
the virtuous and the ugly
we all walked away from the altar pursing our lips
pulling with our blunt tongues at the germ that remained stuck
between tooth and gum.

Long, slow and swaying lines of penitents
walking with bovine grace to our seats, nose to tail.

We have eaten God
and as we stroll to our seats and smile and nod at friends
we clean Him from our teeth.

# END OF SUMMER

*Marion H. Youngquist*

At twilight under twinkling stars
two watch from patio chairs
a firefly ballet dancing
on a rose garden stage
crickets softly beat
their humming rhythms.

She says, *End of August*
shaking ice cubes in a tall glass.
*End of summer*, he sighs.

She frowns—did he say
*summer* or *something?*
Her glass slips falls shatters
splinters with sharp jagged edges.

She turns away,
*Tomorrow, I'll pick up the pieces.*
She moves inside alone.

He stares at the moon—
a pale silver crescent,
a scimitar poised
in a darkening sky.

# The Dust's Cry

*Fran Swarbrick*

Creator God,
　Whose voice didst call
The tranquil clod
　From its dim hall,

Who gave it sight
　That it might bear
The days of light
　In endless glare,

Who woke the stone
　From its cool rest,
And breathed a groan
　Into its breast:

Betray them not
　Who rose in trust
To ache with thought,
　To burn with lust;

Let thy intent
　Steadfast remain,
Lest thou torment
　The dust in vain.

# ADVENT

*Jan Bowman*

Crisp autumn morning
gloved fingers tingle,
frost sprinkled across shingles
stars pierce the midnight-blue sky
each one a sword's point
too far away to threaten us
or release our bonds

unless after years of overcast mornings –
loss after loss piled like thick grey clouds
over the heart's terrain – the beauty
of a single star can lift our gloom
our shrugs of indifference to pain
and stab us with a joy
that bursts from our throats
like a new mother's cry

# Tuesday Afternoon

*Hannah Wallisch*


She is the blue checkered apron
with rick-rack on the pocket,
the box of dog-eared recipe cards,
their gritty coating of flour
rising in puffs as he flips through them,
cards warm against his fingers and thumb.

Outside the kitchen, she is gone.
Her smell faded from the household air,
white soap, sharp and medicinal,
has given way to the musk of old men –
rubber-soled shoes, fried sausage, unshaven cheeks.
As he sits in his worn recliner
to watch an afternoon movie or the daily news,
remote control clutched in his veiny hand,
his elbows graze the solid arms
of threadbare brown corduroy.

But drifting in that place
between waking and sleep,
breath rising in puffs from his parted lips,
those arms are hers.
Her hand lifts the fallen gray hairs
from the collar of his shirt.
Her hum vibrates in the kitchen

His hand reaches for hers
as a sudden noise from the television
jolts him awake.
He shuffles into the kitchen,
strains to ignore the dust on her apron,
its wrinkles from hanging so long untouched.

# AND THEN – NUMBER 2

*Alexander M. Jacobs*

And then there
was the day the hawk
tried to land on the barn peak in the
middle of winter. At the
last moment it saw

the lightening
rod – too late – the wind
had pressed the hawk's back, forcing the belly
down onto the spike. Panic!
The hawk strained to rise

upward, its
head thrashed left, right, back;
wings flailing at the cold air. The wound in
the belly widening until
blood dripped on the barn

peak. The hawk
shrieked. It was hopeless.
In one motion its wings stopped their wild
pattern while the hawk slid down,
impaled on the black

iron spike.
We watched feeling both
fascination and fear. Uncle Frank
ran back into the house to
get the camera.

# Praying For My Enemies

*Eric Huff*

The devil is just a hurt man looking for a friend.
(When did I ever stop praying for my enemies?)
Lord God, please, I ask you, dine with him tonight.
Bring him back to your house and watch a movie.
Share buttered popcorn from under a single blanket.
When the hour is late, take him up in your arms
and lay him down in bed. Pull the covers up to his chin.
Kiss his forehead and wish him pleasant dreams.
Lord, please, the devil is just a hurt man looking for a friend.
In the morning, when he wakes,
greet him with cheer and make him breakfast
and as you stir some cream into his coffee,
ask him how he slept.

# DISTURBED

*Doris Stengel*

I know that voice hallooing at the door.
It wakens me from a lovely nap. Why
can't he let a guy rest? You know,
let sleeping dogs lie and all that rot.

If I get up my sisters are sure to find chores for me.
Life is all priests and politics, death and taxes.
I want to lie here in cool darkness, forget
the demands, the turmoil, to rest my weary bones.

Now my good friend comes, raising his voice,
insisting I rise, just when I am on the verge
of deepest sleep. Tangled in bedclothes
I stumble to the doorway, blinking.

Shading my eyes against the sun I am surprised
I find a crowd gathered. People staring
at me stupefied. What did they expect?
I'd been dead to the world when he called
"Lazarus."

# POET'S LAMENT

*Edward WH Pease*

I can not write tonight.
Nothing comes to mind.

The cool crisp wind
Does caress my skin.
But though she tries
She can not woo me.

The majesty of the church wall
On which I now lean, brings no
Great Truths nor an inner harmony.

The flames that burst
From the October Maples
Can not in their greatest
Attire charm me.

The crow's caw,
The cricket's chirp
Sing no songs to me.

# Confirmation Class

*David Rask Behling*

The old men shuffle into the room;
hair silvered by pale light and their years
falls over heavy lined brows. They move
like scarecrows – wooden and fragile,
with slow and careful steps. Their hands shake
as they carry steaming cups of coffee
to the table. Across from them, boys fidget, whisper,
sip pop, Nikes and Reeboks tucked under chairs.
Smooth, clean faces reflect the light, bodies
slump, glittering eyes flit here and there.
Creaking and squeaking is in the air.
"What does it mean to honor your father and mother?"
the preacher asks. "What does this mean to you?"
The boys roll their eyes like trapped animals,
thinking only of fight or flight when
one man, grey and regal, speaks:
"I wondered about that when I put my parents
in the nursing home. They didn't want to go."
Sudden silence falls over the table.
Grey heads nod, ancient throats clear phlegm,
one mottled hand rises to an eye, drops again.
Adolescent eyes open wide and see tears
on the faces across from them. They sit
still and do not breathe; the world has changed
for them tonight.

# CLEARING OUT

*Dennis Herschbach*

A drawer is opened,
and inside are neatly stacked
scarves and mittens of one
who doesn't live here now.

Time to clear out those ghosts
that lurk in every nook.
Time to pass them on to
those who need warm cover.

But oh how hard it is
to give away a piece
of one's own self,
proof it is now over.

# Catalyst

*Ren Snyder*

We don't need to be scared straight by threats of
apocalypse or promises of streets paved with gold.
We've been through hell and high water, high times
and tall cotton. We've seen and been the good,
the bad and the ugly. We've lived in, and through

Adolescence and teenage angst.  Solitary yearnings
and longings, gropings and gripings, and wanting and
missing.  We remember first blissful, yearning love and the
gospels of sweet front seat kisses, and hot, hot backseat
temptations, and darkness covered outdoor exploring and

Courtship, and solemn vows, and childbirth, and child rearing
and spontaneous mystical couplings in the middle of the night.
We have been baptized in fire and water and in spirit, and have
come from days of scared our parents would catch us, to scared
our kids would catch us, to open celebration and the exhilarating

Rebellion of thinking, catch us if you can. We know about rapture
and tribulation and menopause and insanity and cancer and
    reconciliation.
We have learned the difference between loneliness and solitude.
    And finally,
the difference between looking for perfection in love and
    each other,
and living in love, made perfect by God.

# For Heather's Ordination

*Suzanne S. Schaffer*

Robed in soft cloth,
Ribbons of color round her neck;
Carpenter's wood surrounding and enfolding.
Eyes round with the wonder of life;
Hands reaching, giving touch.
Hearing within those words of eternal time.
This infant of God
Gives voice to communion,
Generation to generation.

Once infant wrappings, now cleric's garb.
Once cradle rocking, now pulpit firm.
Once childhood questioning, now student seeking.
Hearer of God's word and now proclaimer.
Generation to generation.

# Yearly Attitude Adjustment

*Linda M. Johnson*

I'm a fashion statement in jeans and a cotton gown tied at the neck,
while waiting, shivering, for the x-ray tech.
She knocks, walks in, gives a grin and says "Let's get it done."
Face the machine and bare a breast, setting it on a cold, hard shelf.
Placement is critical; she moves it to and fro
while I bemoan the fact they hang so low after
breastfed babes and four decades.
Once I'm in place she says "Face left and hold your breath."
It hurts a little bit, getting squeezed flat
but mammograms save lives, I'm sure of that.
One side complete, x-ray the other.
Finally I'm done for another year!
Overall, the pain is worth it; better safe than sorry.
She leaves, so I shed the gown and get dressed.
While putting on a bra I stop to think.
I'm glad to be alive, and I'm thankful for this day.
I stop and quickly pray.
Thank you, Heavenly Father,
for all of my blessings,
for health care, and medical tests.
Thank you for making me a woman.
A woman with breasts.

# PLAIN ASSURANCE

*Jennifer Zarth*


You awake with a start at 3 am
on a black December night
left alone in the world
You want something to hold onto

Is God in the corner of the cotton
sheet you grasp like a baby's tight fist around a lovey?

Will you find God in the intricate lace of bitter frost
on the cold window?

Maybe God is in the bills and letters on the corner desk,
the antique silver letter opener,
plastic snowglobe and brass drawer pull

Even as you walk around the darkened room like a lost angel,
rumpled from a frightened sleep,
and touch of all of this,
unkind glass on the mirror, the white stitching of your gown,
you look for God's secret imprint

Now think of a time
as a girl on Christmas night,
a bell ringing in the distance,
your hand slipped inside your father's gloved hand,
as he fumbled with the keys on the
snowy front steps,
a single high star overhead that promised plain assurance
and – sleep.

# Pasture colt

*Diane Scholl*

He gives a name to grief, with his spindly legs
that tremble in the sharp cold of early April.
When he's surprised on his dry bed of leaves,
he whinnies for his mother, grazing against
the distant trees at sunset.  She answers curtly,
turns to some pressing purpose she does not confide.
All day in the field he stands beside her nursing,
or, when the spirit takes him, game as the spring
wears on, runs over tufts and knobby hills
to his pasture pond, the waiting block of salt.
This might be forever, he thinks, this lark in thin,
brilliant air outlined by tender green.  One evening
he's gone, the white star like his mother's
a sudden gap in the symmetry of earth and sky,
an edge keen as winter in the landscape's aching dark.

# Communion

*Dick Stahl*

The Mississippi River starts a spirit
that always moves me
to transcendence
and faith.  Look at the sun-filled troughs
of waves that work from source
to mouth, from shore to shore, making
a new channel of stippled light
every second.  Sometimes, on foggy mornings,
the river seems hidden, distant, cold and dead,
but I know it's working harder
than ever, and once this spring shroud's lifted,
there lies the whole truth
of the matter, the whole and resurrected body
of the risen one.  This is the moment
my eyes drop
into the eddies and whirlpools and sinking sands
of the Rock Island Rapids.  Beware the power
of the undertow and bless
its quick running.  I see the unseen,
and here's the clear water
that washes over me.

# Summer Night

*Constance E. Ciway*

Wrapped in
butter crème eyelet
I sat in my turtle-shaped sandbox
and watched the stars wake.
The sky the color of blushing orchids,
I wandered barelegged
in the wet, black grass,
reaching white star-shaped hands
to the rising fireflies.
I held them carefully
as they illuminated my face.
But the older neighborhood boys
ran on the sidewalk
and crushed the fireflies beneath
heavy sneakers, fleeing
with cold laughter.
Bitterly I cried as I reached
for their bodies.
I could not wipe the neon blood
from my trembling fingers.
Daddy came to carry me home,
a shaking yellow crocus.

# Sharing Caleb's Dream

*Arlet Osnes Vollers*

Give me a mountain, Lord,
To climb where I can view
Sunrise, sunset, waterfall,
Vistas – wide and new;
Where I can find the higher path,
My destiny,
Above the level plain
Of mediocrity.
I need the struggle too,
From it new life will flow
As sense is sharpened,
Spirit renewed, insights grow…
Though I may falter from hot sun,
Weariness, fear
Of falling rock, mis-step,
I know you will be near.
And when I reach the top
With fog and clouds behind,
Having slain giants
That limit body, soul, and mind;
Ahead will lay my promised land,
A steady beam
Leading me, like Caleb,
As God fulfills my dream.

# SPRING MELT

*Ann Boaden*

Long pools of wet
mud
yellow ruck and rivulet
of winter grit;
old leaves
like rust flakes;
wandering basketry
of sticks;
stone chips;
squashed blue glitter
of unrecycled cans;
filter tips
from smoked-out cigarettes;
old seed pods like the cast-off spines
of fish –
what a mish-mash.
What a mess.

With snow and ice the surfaces are smooth,
still and cold as cream;
blossoms
on shivering twigs;
bolsters
for crooked bones of branch;
and there is majesty
in crystal arrows
that steady, shape,
and point
the weeping of our eaves.

No wonder then
that some of us
prefer the freeze.

# THE FEELING OF SILENCE

*Matthew Kruse*

in a world filled with cacophonies of voices, sound, noise
time quickly fleeting,
smells of fear, tastes of success
i do not think of what it means to feel.

a breath, a pause
my worries and anxieties release
as silence reflects life's reality.
i reach beyond myself to hear the echoes of my true voice
hidden beneath humdrum
i feel.

detached from the world's expectations,
my heart bellows in deep reflection
life: honest joys, violent pangs, choking death,
its truths and lies
intense silence
God.

the voice is a precious thing to share
absence of voice exposes wounds of the true voice concealed
my truest despairs escape

silence is not heard, but felt
peace: the release of a million silent screams.

# LETTING GO

*Norma Thorstad Knapp*

The judge's decree signed,
I went to the church where we wed,
sat in a pew, praying, pondering
on the ways you had hurled hurt –
betraying, deceiving,
breaking sacred vows –
eons of secret making.


Remembering myriad broken promises,
I folded like a rag doll
into a wailing heap,
stroking my wedding band
while Biblical words of forgiveness
bounced about sanctuary walls.


Attempting to discharge
anger, resentment, bitterness,
I drove to my apartment
and buried one room with balloons
filled with hot air – like you.


Later I scribbled my feelings
onto each one.
And added *thankful* –
for children and grandchildren.


Outside, I released each balloon,
gently, one at a time,
turning them over to the Father.

# fried rolls

*Bradley Allen Froslee*

inga's fried rolls
served to brothers
dueling on swivel stools
lined against a formica counter
in a small town cafe
as elders drink coffee
collecting tidbits on
the weather, the nation,
church, and neighborhood gossip
that ages as red wine
more flavorful by the minute.

milk washes down the rolls
adding nutrition to the
diet as old men continue
to muse and moan
as old men sometimes do
with one chewing snuse
and spitting in a can
wiping his chin clean as
the two boys dab their
faces with cheap paper
napkins licking their lips
to absorb the last bit of
sugar glaze left by
inga's fried rolls.

# Untitled

*David Melby-Gibbons*

All the magnetic poets I've met.
In puffy wool vests and dented thin hats,
they wear their cares and sharp sounds
with a clap of laughter that catches the throat
and measures the distance from here to what matters.
And they reassure with perspiring arms,
at length they reach eight feet and walk as eagles
fitted to the circles of devotion
that hold them up and keep us waiting.

# ROPE

*J.L. Bond*

heels dig in
body at a tilt
palms burn
with sweat dirt blood
I pull on the rope
a tug-of-war
my way versus the Almighty's

for hours I drag
and twist
until the Spirit yanks
at my will
anger frays
grip slackens
body bends

I braid submission
trust and peace
drawn into
the lariat of His love

# Wearing the Robe

*Jessica Rivera*

Who am I...
I wonder this sometimes
mostly on Sunday mornings,
As I sit uncomfortably in the high backed chair
looking at red-painted toes in my favorite high heels
Poking out from underneath the white-robe of my position

I wonder at this when eyes travel to wonder at my earrings
As I speak earnestly of faith
When I am introduced as the "girl Pastor" to visitors
who shake my hand and say
"Wow, I've never had a girl before, You're pretty good"
As if this was surprising because I was born
with different parts than they expected
To be wearing this white-robe

In my secret chats with God I ask the question
and wonder about dating and children
"I am a woman" I say to God "can I be a lover and a pastor too?"
Or does love require a quiet and demure woman
instead of a preacher?
And does the white robe fit over 9 months pregnant belly?

God answers my question
Not always on Sunday morning
But always quietly, almost mischievously when
whispered conversations in sleeping bags lead to thoughts of Jesus
When babies cry at warm water embrace faith
When harmony breaks loose in wooden pews, lifting faith song
And call comes clear in bright colors
You are my chosen one, God says
And white-robe becomes swaddling cloth of becoming
instead of the bondage
of my position.

# Storm Warning

*Lynda M. Maraby*


Silence
and the dropping curtain
of a late December

Herod's forces
regroup
for one last offensive
from a horizon
obscured.

Ensconced in tinsel
and tradition,
we scurry
to whatever
beckons

hoping for inward grace,
searching for outward signs,
distracted

by all the pretty lights.

# DREAD

*Raymond E. Hartung*

Ideals billowing softly, but still they are silent.
Dried leaves stir in windless memory's eye.
An eerie draft of air unable to relent,
Oft teach human-dreams to fly.

A dearth of nature's music rides the currents.
Soulfully melancholy, but alas tragically askew.
In morning sunlight, burnished fruit hangs listlessly.
Mindful of its fate, a human clue.

And so in life, the labors of all women,
Live on by some precarious thread.
Where daily, heartaches are rend asunder,
What comes is often more than dread.

# A Complex Music

*Ellen Roberts Young*

Breath of God
in snowflakes, coral,
in water dripping
through branches.

Human breath
spoils its own past
and future: Lascaux,
an angry mother's child.

God's breath sings
the tears of children,
kicked cats, birds dazed
by glass windows,

the respiration
mingled with steam
from a heat vent
under torn blankets.

# SPRING

*Karen Cornish*

Pied Piper Spring leaps
      to the march
dances over tender blades of
      green young grass
hop-skippity-scotch
      cart wheel turns
and whirls a coat of crocuses yellow
      and tulip tips
to the fluttering notes that tingle in the
      sweet, new air.

# OF DEATH AND RESSURRECTION

*John Hulteen*

I saw a rose bedecked in bloom,
Few days ago or so it seems.
Her petals soft in pink and white,
Her green leaves done in artists' schemes.

Life for her was light and gay,
As summer winds blow softly now
And butterflies and bees fly down
To rest their wings upon her brow.

But summertime has troubles, too,
With thunderstorms and wind-whipped rain
To test the very faith she has,
That roots, set deep, can stand the strain.

Yet certain as the summer ends,
The prairie winds turn harsh and cold;
In endless sweeps across the plains.
Her strength must stay; her roots must hold.

The prairie rose is silent now;
Her leaves lie dead upon the ground.
The winds blow through her barren boughs
With a strange and lonesome whistling sound.

Though winter's death consumes her now,
Like waters rushing to the sea,
The prairie rose will bloom again;
And so shall we - and so shall we.

# Creation

*Lois Batchelor Howard*

God took the brown
And sculpted it…
  Foundation
He took the blue
And breathed into it…
  Sky
He took the velvet
And scrunched it…
  Mountains
He took the green
And lifted it…
  Trees
He took the blue-green
And gave it depth…
  Oceans, lakes, rivers
He took the colorless Spirit…
And starfully made
  Each Me

# FAITH

*Cathryn A. Spelts*


The tom-tom beat of Faith
  echoes in my thoughtful meditation,
    pulsing courage
      into my clouded mind.

Once Future seemed so loud and luring,
  drumming excitement with every stroke.
As silently as engulfing fog, Future has
  slipped into a calming cadence,
Offering the softened, steady beat of
  now, now, now, now—

The rhythm of Faith is most sufficient.

# SCANDINAVIAN MOTHERS
(for Catherine Pederson and Edna Liljegren)

*Alice M. Azure*


Cold winter sun pouring
through these calico curtains of
red and green,
cold winter sun lighting on
pot holders with nubby roses of
red and green –
woven thick
to protect her rough hands
from ovens too hot,
my mother crocheted beauty
in opposite hues

like my second mother
who gathered this cloth,
the threads of her life
contained in old patterns,
impossible tensions of
opposite hues.

My mothers, in love
I give you thanks;
who'd ever think
curtains and pot holders
would give to my kitchen
that certain elusory
designer's touch?

# THE SOWER PARAPHRASED

*Scott Wayne Hamre*


A sower went to sow some seed
in a story Jesus told
Dropping seed upon the fallow ground
in hopes of harvest gold.
Some seed fell on the road and died
some seed fell in the stone
some seed fell out among the thorns
where the incessant world beat drones.
Some seed fell splendid in the rich good soil
and, there, grew tall and bold
and when the sower came to reap
produced a hundred-fold.
Now in this hurried, tragic world
we're all seeds in the thorn
lives woven deep, intractably,
from the day that we are born -
though in good soil we may hope to be
we must not lose our heart
but do that which we know we must
and let God do God's part.

# SONG FOR GINA

*Dave Brauer-Rieke*


Beneath the star lit heavens –
-   wind,
the ripening of time,
God's Spirit stirring here within
our walls of space and rhyme
with memories
-   of those now gone,
-   of mystery and fear,
with memories
-   of bread and wine
-   of joys and pain too dear.


So from our hearts a Sister Song,
with words that cannot speak.
A prayer for one who, like us all,
Sin's ravages doth reap –
-   beneath the star lit heavens…


wind,
-   a prayer,
-   a song,
-   a canticle of hope and calm,
Awaiting from the hand of God
a gift of Grace –
-   beyond the star lit heavens.

# NIGHTTIME VISITORS

*Sherry Knight Rossiter*

Gliding silently, gracefully,
across the snow-packed sod,
the night visitors came,
full of hope.
Intent on finding nourishment,
the dung-brown hides
stake out their turf.

Two young elk
momentarily play
King of the Hill
while the others continue to forage,
uninterested in empty challenges.

Winter clouds marshal overhead
as the moon plays hide and seek.
Even freeway noise
fails to deter the beasts
from their satiate mission.

Then, as if predetermined,
the dark bodies move stealthily
up the slope only to disappear
over the ridge from where they came,
away from the winking lights and
waking households below,
hoof marks streaming in the snow
the only reminder of nighttime visitors.

# Bird Feeders

*Linda J. Hommes*

Mom's fragile frame
sits cradled by the high-backed chair
as she watches the birds
flitting at the feeders
outside our window

"Fill the bird feeders"
her voice chatters at me
as does the feisty red squirrel
when I annoy him
by my presence at the window
She thinks I've nothing else
to do with my life
but fill bird feeders

Now she sits
in another home
her space tightly drawn
half a shared room
chartreuse curtain separating lives
no window
to see the birds

"Fill the bird feeders"
her voice echoes in my memory
the same refrain
as I pass the window we once shared
wishes not granted
what I could have done
when she asked me.

# THE IMAGE OF GOD

*Roy B. Wingate*

Listen to the piano music
Rise with ecstatic ease,
Music rung from wood and wire
By racing fingers.
Our God was wise to form man with hands
To match the piano keys.
So formed must God be, if man is in His image.

# VEILED ACTUALITY

*David Reiman*

Beneath these jaded eyes,
Whose gloss reflect the sky,
They've discovered us,
And they have unraveled the lie.

Toward the commotion,
As if a jewel lay in our incentive,
Why did it matter,
For the dream to stay alive?

God watches us,
As the pitch white sky blinds,
To live for an unseen entity,
Is faith and subliminal desire.

Art left behind,
A comforting cliché,
Creating the untruth,
Of the aura today.

With our structure of glass,
Failing to resist the wind,
Only the beauty of renown,
Is found in a human mind.

The ambience surrounds,
And light and the sound,
With only a whisper and bread,
A direct connection is found.

Complexity of a world,
A world made to be,
A world to withstand,
The lies unseen.

# [untitled]

*Donna Beth Nelson*

There is a crack I keenly want to go
      through.
It leads upstairs where all things come
      and all things go.
It's a very vulnerable and auspicious
      place to be,
For many want to go along, but can't
      feasibly, you know.


It's where the words mingle endlessly
      for the poems,
And where the colors mutate into
      prisms;
Where the melodies are, when you are
      half awake,
With vernal vegetation and abundant
      fruit to take.

# Hiding Together with a Three Year Old

*Andy Rutrough*

Underneath a ten-dollar royal blue sleeping bag,
I pretend to swim beneath the sea.
Looking down, I try to show you gobies,
sea anemones and silver flashing fish.
You will have none of it.
Intensely, you enforce our hiddeness
with wild, inarticulate joy.
We are completely unseen, not there.
At three, you have circumvented
your instinctive fear of death
and glanced beyond the grave.
What is it like to be gone?
Or is being gone not really being gone,
but rather being inside the womb;
unseen, warm, enclosed
in quivering wonder?

# Night Fishing

*Anders Dovre*

The moon drags its pale cape across the water,
Shining on lovers scraping their skin across sand,
Joining goose bumps and spider bites in the shallows,
While my line dangles in the deep.

# The Meaning of Life is a Moment

*Caty Heyn*

When I stand on a clear spring morning,
back against a sun-warmed wall,
the meaning of life is tangled
within the waves of hair
which I smooth between my fingers.

When I sit upon a woolen blanket
stretched across sand twilight-cool,
the meaning of life is sinking away
with the sun as it is exhausted
by the passionate kisses of the sea.

When I lie beside you half asleep,
bodies braided in quiet warmth,
the meaning of life is hushed
by the rise and fall of breath
that gives life hope.

I've struggled for years to believe
there is more to life than this,
but there are only these moments —
joy and pain that break my heart
with their clarity.

# untitled

*Katie Bombardi*

where do I belong?
isn't it strange how I would be able to fit into many places
yet there is no place I call my own?
i don't even know if I could live in Ohio over California
new York over Kentucky
it's not that I'm looking for a place to live
but rather a place to
hide

you know, where no one thinks you're
strange
or out of place
you fit with something.
anything.
maybe that's why I like cities so much
everyone fits
and at the same time
no one belongs

having no connection with anything in particular
you can find bits of yourself
everywhere.

# First Prayers

*Paul Shepherd*


a first prayer,

for wanting no more words
than the man who drove his truck into a snowdrift
and lived for a month, writing notes to his wife
on every scrap of paper he could find,

a second prayer,

for things that grow too much,
mondo and nandina, the pestilence,
for what I know that I have killed,
– some of it I can not name –

a third prayer,

for an end of prayer,
no long moments with this God,
who hears what is forgot,
who folds in a thousand neglects,

a first prayer, not to say.

# STORM DOOR

*Joan Wiese Johannes*

When the house became so hot
we couldn't breathe,
my parents dragged the storm door
down the steps of our front porch,
their cheeks pressed together
with the heavy pane between.
On the swing, my little sister sat
so still her legs hung
like a fraction of a spider.

In an inchworm of a voice,
she told me Dad had sworn
to take us to the woods
and beat the daylights out of us
if we were bad again
now that the neighbors could hear us
through the scream door.

I thought of telling her
she hadn't heard him right, but didn't.

# THE CHILD WITHIN

*Wayne L. Quam*

Are we children still in bodies grown
Aged by the will of God alone?
Or is it time, no beginning no end,
That ages and our bodies to offend?
Or do we progress at nature's whim
From birth to life's last requiem?
It matters not by what course we age,
The end is set, though at time we rage.
What matters then if God's will be done
Or time prevail or nature's won?
Is the child within our saving grace,
Who lives for the day, this time, this place?
A child inside tempers aging's pace
And wonders at life without disgrace.
Youth gives way under aging's press
To withdraw from the body's outer dress
To find its safety in the mind
And free our hearts from ages crime.

# OLD FRIEND

*Christie Nielsen*

Beautiful and rich is an old friendship,
Grateful to the touch as ancient ivory.
Smooth as aged wine or sheen of tapestry
Where light has lingered, intimate and long.
Full of tears and warm is an old friendship
That asks no longer deeds of gallantry,
Or any deed at all - save that the friend shall be
Alive and breathing somewhere, like a song.

# The Deer of Otter Cliff

*Barbara Focht Dorgan*

Behold, the deer of Otter Cliff is slain…
That was the word; I quickly grabbed my hat
That I might be protected from the rain…
The thunder broke; the sky was dark and flat.

And as I came upon the scene, I smelled
The scent of pine where once I saw him frolic;
I wondered if perhaps a maddened Celt
Had done this act, half crazed from gruesome tonic.

Blowing across the deer, the wind turned sour…
Rain on his lifeless form caused it to glisten;
Some others came and left within the hour…
I stood by the deer, took off my hat, and listened

To sounds of rain and sadness all in fusion;
The deer that I loved was real…all else illusion.

# Prayer

*Robert Cording*

Forgive me,
but I must imagine you

for my sake
without comfort, always

suffering what we cannot help,
it seems, but do.

I must imagine the massacre
of the innocent always in your eyes;

And I must imagine every cry,
every siren, every gunshot
as a hurricane in your ear;

I must have the smell of carrion
stuffing your nostrils,

and the raw taste of horror
always on your tongue;

Forgive me,
but I cannot imagine you

without imagining your flesh –
every inch of you must be

tattooed with the dirty-needle
history of human misery.

# All Along

*Susan D. Gordon*

Just when the rain seems to have been falling forever
And the gray of the sky seems indelibly etched,
The warmth of the sun sneaks through
And the corners of your heart are filled with sparkling promise.
Just when it feels like the world has forgotten your address
And your phone seems to have been silent far too long,
The calendar does not hold enough days
And the hours fly by with alarming speed..
Just when you wonder how to start.
You cannot find the time to think of stopping
And the essence of life itself fills every moment
As magic memories melt together
Just when you cannot decide what to do or where to go,
When plans long made seem far out of reach
And you stare at what was thought to be the only way out,
The road ahead opens clear and inviting
And life itself becomes one with you again.
Just when becomes now and ever
And on you go
To greener pastures and brighter skies
Along paths that have been here all along.

# MARRIAGE SCAN

*Mary Margaret Rode*

Always the skeptic
My grandmother said
She hoped it would work
(In dubious tones).
Fifty-two years now and
I wish she could see us
Surprisingly welded together
Amazingly proud of one another
Dare I say loving?
Respectful and disrespectful
Agreeing and disagreeing
Dependent and independent
Running the gamut of years
Sometimes stumbling
Over sharp rocks
But holding on to each other.

# Hush

*Melinda Graham*

I have no tears
shed the measure of a lifetime
in a salt sea on my pillow
I am parched    ragged
blood thick in lazy veins

high above my bed
a wide sweep of window
hangs quiet with white lace
stilled in the afternoon heat
I wonder if I am alive
as the sun settles west

a sigh born at the horizon
moves slow across the earth
whispers through the window
to promenade the threadwork
arc and billow of a waltz
fills the sky of my room
fretwork patterns shift across
my dusky evening skin

despite myself I breathe
rise and fall    breast and belly
a thump from a hesitant heart

# DUST – ASH WEDNESDAY

*Frank A. Vollmer*

Does the wind know
The value of the dust
It whirls into a column
Is it trying to make a man
If it succeeded
Would it blow its creation away
On a whim
Would it love its creation
Would it die for him
Would it hover over him
Like a mother hen
Fussing forgiving
Time and again
Folding him to her bosom
Or would it
As so many gods but One
Fade falter
And go away

# Anointed

*Dale P. Chesley*

Bitterly cold;
Christmas Eve Day;
A committal at a windy North Dakota prairie cemetery.

Our broken hearts suffered the weather appropriate.

A nineteen year old daughter.
A holiday tragedy.
A late night rollover.

It felt right to freeze while we buried her.

Her father is a tall man.
I am short.
My arm his waist, his arm my shoulders.

At the car he turned and kissed my forehead.

I wasn't embarrassed.
I know it wasn't planned.
I felt anointed.

Few things as genuine and warm have been in me so deeply planted.

The man I sought to comfort
Reached out to me with human touch.
We stood against the cold.

Shadowed in this face I saw the suffering of Christ.

# Red Tide

*Nancy Payne*

When we were here last,
The sea was warm and clean.
My lover sat in the playful surf,
bounced and tickled by the waves.

Now, like forgotten tissues,
silver fish lie at the tide line
among the shells.
Ignored by the sated gulls,
Glimmering in the falling rain.
The air is harsh with
throat-scratching red tide.

A plankton population explosion –
Marine folk have learned
to deal with it by avoiding it
like the grief that grips my heart.

The sea doesn't look red.
It should be ugly and harsh.
It should be hateful and vicious.
It should rise out of the mist
like a beast, drooling slime,
frightening lonely humans,
stalking birds and sea creatures.

Instead, it's merely eerily sad.

# TO TOUCH THE RAT

*Amy Grogan*

The rat moves from stomach
  to sternum. I grab its body,
  clumped beneath my shirt.
Rapid rat breaths pulse under my hand,
  rat body squirms. Fear starts.
If I let go, will the rat fly in my face,
  or burrow down deeper?
How long can I hold the rat,
  just so?

What would it be like
  to touch the rat?
Would I feel soft rat fur,
  a skinny rat tail,
  delicate touch of rat whiskers,
  or slice of rat teeth?
Would a dark rat eye stare me down?
Would rat claws tear into my flesh,
  leaving a trace of rat scars?

My hold slackens.
The rat is still.
Cautiously, I pull back my shirt,
  reach in but feel no fur, no whiskers,
  just a lump beneath my stretched skin.

# WINTER AT THE BEACH

*Richard F. Bansemer*

Grayer skies than artists paint
Fill the sea with woes,
Except for foam six wide waves deep
As white as mountain snows.

The muffled roar of tide and surf
Behind the looking pane
Is heard above the splashing sky
Unleashing heavy rain.

Those creepy waves look menacing
When lined up row on row
To eat the sandy beach for sport
As rain now turns to snow.

No children play with sand or pail,
No lovers walk alone.
The cold and gray prepare the days
For them to know, for each to own.

Since God began creation's toil
Each day combines to make this now
Through earthquake, wind and white hot fire.
All artists bend, in reverence bow.

# MOONLIT

*Michael E. Jenkins*

Through dark of night, the moon, in full, regards
All lives complete, from laughter unto tears.
And you, full too, enfold with steadfast arms
A life called mine these past, peculiar years.
With love as constant as the faithful moon,
You tend our fire as bellows, sure and strong.
In dark of fear, so close around, we soon
Will glow, intense; refining all that's wrong.
Aturn toward dawn, and look, the moon is still
Alit:  daymoon of subtle benevolence.
Though pale and small, you still have strength to spill
Your light and life on my world, dark and dense.
In places low, you gather in a pool,
And I am awash in moonlight – your light – pure and cool.

# PRAYER IN A CYNICAL AGE

*Kate Walters*

Pray!  They say and how do you answer this…
How do I explain that original sin isn't the beginning or the end
but maybe just some stories to explain why…
I pray.
Though I had to run from God to find him…
I pray.
Though I am prodigal and prostate,
Pious and pissed off and Ready to go in Any direction…
Except half of them are forbidden,
and fun.
I pray.
I am the student of intellectual atheists and still…
I pray.
I am too many hours deciding this must be fake and still…
I pray.
I am angry and arrogant,
Embarrassed and humble and Searching in Any direction
Cause I forgot which ones are forbidden.
Held tight lover and scripture says its sin and still…
I pray.
The pious ones make me nervous and still…
I pray.

One small voice, seeking and finding,,,
What blessing this is.
Will I ever stop resisting?
I pray.

# THE COLORS OF LOVE

*Elizabeth J. Leopard*


It's as white as thin starlight on new fallen snow,
Or gray as a wind throwing fists full of sleet at the night.

It's as red as blood from a wounded heart that breaks,
or as blue as the inside of a dream.

Do the winds of Love blow icy across a clear night,
biting tender petals, turning roses to rust,
or does it rise gently on the breeze,
soft as a baby's cheek
nestled against her mother's breast?

The colors of Love are seen in the fabric of life;
God provides the canvas; mankind adds the color.

# Two Sonnets For My Brother's Ordination

*Mark Bouzard*

I.
A Sunday morn, no different than the rest.
Mankind pauses, breaks the bread, sips the wine
And trundles homeward to whatever best
Is on the tube. Again there was no sign
From God, no voice from the sky announcing
His full and loving ardor for all men,
Secular torper once again pouring
Water on flames which fall on coals within.

A mighty fortress is our God! – Equal
In might must his shepherds be; providence
Seeks arsonist to tend his sheep. To pull
Sloth faith to zeal, His word to sustenance.
Let him strengthen speech, deeds, faith, life and art.
His will be done by stout loving heart.

II.
Three stones tossed in a still pond will ripple
Ever outwards; their intersection
A model for the Trinity. Simple
Solution to centuries of debate. Son,
Father, and Holy Ghost spread forth bound
Only by the pool's edge. From there they race
Back, collide, and all at once without sound
The pond dances: living emblem of grace.

Should we in our strength confide, water
Would ripple for each stone tossed in its depth.
But the Master asks more; not just to stir
Pools but in faith to walk resultant crests.
Souls and stones communicate in this thing;
When tossed in pond both justified by Ring.

# Fear Unveiled – Ely, MN

*Mark Patrick Odland*

The tangled ebony of branching trees
Shrivels into the clod – withering
Effortlessly brushed aside crumpled canvass Red Sea
The moon above shattering its luminous silver slivering

Wind gusts through the aluminum of chimes and crack
Bone breaking chatter of dogs and citizens sleep oblivious
Street lamps flicker buzz hum go black
The galloping of distant riders' crescendo looms insidious

# Thoughts on September 11, 2001

*Winifred M. Sawrun*

The smoke curls upward
A massive funeral pyre for 3000 innocents.
The heavens have been dry for days
Tears of the mourners run rivers into the soil.
The once towering symbols of a mighty empire now mere powder.
Torn metal, twisted by some tormented giant leans in space.
A single flag waves gently.
And stillness reigns.

# Peace Be With You

*Donna Simmons*


*Dear Friend…Very Truly Yours,*
*Hi there…Sincerely.*
*Peace be with you…And with you, too,*
*Go in Peace, Serve the Lord…*
*Thanks be to God.*

Rituals of our culture and faith,
the routine we take for granted.
At least I did, until the state trooper
drove into our dooryard
to tell us our son was dead.
Nothing was going to be *dear*
or *very truly ours* again.
God was never going to grant me *peace*…again.

Through darkness, grief and depression
I saw the standard greetings
I had said throughout my life
were now truly without meaning.

When I came back to church
*Sharing The Peace* took me by surprise.
A lifeline was thrown
and I was reminded that God
works through kindness and compassion
of strangers and of friends.

The person's hand you are shaking
may need the lifeline you offer;
or you may be the one searching for the meaning
behind the gesture:
*Peace Be With You…Go With God.*

# THE ELKHORN VALLEY

*Carlita L. Pedersen*

Have you ever seen the valley
Where the Elkhorn River flows?
Have you seen it in the evening
When the day begins to close?

Have you seen it from a hilltop
When the purple shadows play
Across the fields and meadows
In a lazy sort of way?

Have you seen the red-winged blackbirds
Perched on reedy sprigs of grass?
Have you heard the larks a'singing
From the fence rows as you pass?

Have you seen the night descending
Across the darkening earth
And felt the smallness of yourself
And wondered at your worth?

Have you heard the booming silence
That echoes from the hill
When the sun has settled for the night
And time is standing still?

If you have, you've seen the beauty
Which man cannot portray
In the valley of the Elkhorn
At the closing of the day.

# GIVEN FREE REIGN

*Jeffrey Johannes*


Eve scribbles on the beach in Eden,
stirring sand back and forth,
imagining the many possibilities.

The movement of her hand
and arm and body satisfies
something deep inside.

Before her is a seamless creation
of her own making.
She sketches a sky-lit studio

in Santa Fe where she can write
poetry about the fate of snakes
and paint pictures of apples

because they are beautiful and round.
God knows she will leave soon,
buy a motorcycle and race toward

cocktail parties and galleries
with intriguing conversations
about knowledge and desire

and the complexity of being both
woman and myth.

# To Joey

*Connie Krueger*

Blessed child of my child,
prayed-for gift from God,
now marked with the cross of Christ
forever.

Spirit-filled baby boy,
reborn in water.
New life, freely given,
forever.

Innocent believer
kingdom inheritor,
forsaken never, loved
forever.

# SNIPPET

*Barbara Crooker*

That mockingbird's going jabber, jabber, jabber;
doesn't he ever shut up?  Early June, and the peonies
have finally opened; they nod their pink heads
in the soft sweet wind.  The afternoon begins
to blossom, the air like table syrup, the lawn,
a bowl of sunshine.  From far off, a woodpecker
is knocking, knocking.  Batter my heart, three-
personed God, dip it in flour, salt, and milk;
fry it up, good and golden as this afternoon,
one shining lake of light.

# Dancing Closer to God

*Kera Béh*

Tiny white feet
Dance across the moonlit, rain-soaked grass
She tilts her face up to the velvety blackness
(Mother is telling her that she will catch her death of cold)
She is wrapped in God's love
Each splash on her face driving her passion deeper
She is dancing
For and with
Her Maker and true Father
(Earthly father is yelling that *normal* children are scared silly of
    thunderstorms)
Thunderstorms don't frighten her
The thunder is just God laughing at the latest theory from
    evolutionists
In fact, He's laughing so hard He's
Crying
The lightning is just His
Teeth flashing in a grin
Against His dark face
(Her parents are nearly hoarse
With shouting at her to come inside)
She stretches her arms up to heaven
Gripping her heavenly Father's fingers
As He whirls her about
"I'm sorry my parents don't understand."
Thunder.
"Go inside.
We can play some more tomorrow."
She laughs and
After a last whirl
Races inside
Already thinking about
Tomorrow night's
Dance.

# INSPIRATION

*Elayne Clipper Hanson*

I wrapped spring around me
while apple and plum trees
bloomed their fragrance,
lilacs scented my senses.
Pansies nodded welcome
and sent their brilliant hues
to rest behind my eyes
where memory lodges.
Trees preened green,
a backdrop of support
and envy,  and
I walked barefoot
through fields of poems.

# Corn

*Laura Hirneisen*


Mine is gone, stolen by the farmer
whose name is, of all things, Daniel Boone,
not the historic settler but bald and fat,
a seventyish man in work boots
who drives his Chrysler into the field
to check kernels for his steer.
Taken in a daily theft, first this row
then the next next next until all stalks
wave ragged ends in concession,
shorn like a fever patient's hair.
Empty patches with dirt, a fox who stalks
voles, shrews, his smaller prey
along a peripheral route, afraid
maybe he too will be taken,
ribs picked clean, spare teeth left
on his vulture-poked skull days later.

# I Learn to Dance

*Peggy Rushton*


My Father's hands
held strength
and punishment.
Gloved in
fine blond hairs
clipped and clean,
they dwarfed his coffee cup.

Calloused patience,
made rough
by the steel they carried.
He carried me, sometimes.
His hands met
around my waist
and easily lifted me
onto broad shoulders.

When I was five years old,
he rolled the living room rug
to one side,
and stood me on his shoes
to teach me
the four smooth counts
of the fox-trot.

When that music lifted
through heavy July air,
I danced
so very light.

# Reformation

*Arnie Johanson*

My friends all wanted to be Superman
when they grew up.  I wanted to be Martin Luther,
a fortress for the Lord, standing strong
against the Pope and all his wicked priests.
I'd slay them with the truth. I'd shout God's Word,
rescuing Rome's victims from the mouth of hell.
I'd take on Lucifer himself, like Luther did,
but my ink wouldn't miss its mark.

I did stand up before the Pope one day, stared
squarely in his eyes through my Kodak Pony.
He looked like Uncle Frank, chubby, gray,
a smile that nobody could ever want to fight.
I shared good Lutheran beer with priests I met.
They did not try to trick me into deeding
my possessions and posterity to the Holy See.
I never found the monsters Mother warned me of.

I could still do battle with the devil, I suppose.
He's never shown himself to me in any form
that I could throw things at. He may have been
a partner in some projects I pursued. It's hard
to fight an enemy who lurks inside your skin,
especially when you kinda like the lurking.
And the sword of truth is useless when its edge
gets blunted by confusion and despair.

I never will be Luther.  But my friends
can't even leap short buildings in single bounds.
We go on being who we are.  God help us.

# Demi-Gog

*Charles Strietelmeier*

They stared, and he misread
The tense amazement in their faces.
Were they struck dead
By his great phrases -
Toppling from thick lips,
The heavy words that fell
Like lamps and tables thrown
Around a room once restful?

No, they were just amazed
That anyone could make
The truth so ugly.
His deep voice razed.
He drove his point
Squarely in their eyes -
The moving finger jabbed,
And scrabbled on.

# CREDO

*John Alexanderson*

Two roses on autumn's slope,
a Pennsylvania backlot's breeze.

Single petals frolic pink like kids at play,
wizen canes lurch as old men might,

ache for June to tint at leisure once again.
Where does color go when leaflets crisp

and drop like chips? When lifeblood
hunkers low as stems dispel to sticks?

When warm noon élan retreats from fronds
and few remain to jitter down the wind?

Today, indian summer fables frost-veined
earth and ice that skulks in weeks ahead.

And yet, this fathom pink asserts return
Upon its chosen bloom rebirth in Spring.

# The Vigil of Easter

*Stephen C. Bond*

Today the sun did not awaken,
God-with-us lies godforsaken.
Father, your own Son was taken –
Where are you while earth is shaken?
It seems, amid the silent tears,
He is not here.

Tonight disciples still are scattered
Nature groans and faith is battered.
Darkened cave and linens, tattered,
Hold the body, broken, shattered.
Within the cold and hollow fear
He is here.

We bring before the light of morning
Spices for one last adorning,
Stunned by angels without warning,
Folded graveclothes end our mourning,
With good news sung out loud and clear:
"He is not here!"

Our Hope is risen, not exhumed
He made the grave itself a womb.
While all the world waits in this room,
Between the cross and empty tomb,
The Risen Lord stays ever near:
He is here!

# WALKING

*Riitta Passananti*

under the gauzy canopy
of may woods
I search for the spot where
ladyslippers used to bloom
on a sundappled hillside

a friend meets me
with a bevy of beloved beasts
they chase in wide circles
through the tender underbrush
race after sticks and shake
wet shaggy coats at our feet

we fall in step
tracing familiar patterns
on the pine needle-cushioned ground
we think each other's thoughts
smile at the happy barking
echoing in the trees

the path runs into the road
the past crashes into today
I turn to wave
they stay behind
ghost dogs   ghost friend
they wait

# THE DARK NIGHT OF GETHSEMANE

*Tiffany Demke*

Silence stirred a soul to weep,
from depths so deep senses ceased,
piercing truth on bended knees,
secrets whispered in prayer received.

Illumined gaze in dark of night,
pleas of sorrow this cup to pass,
the Son of Man embraced a kiss,
and crowed the cock in Peter's ear.

Scattered sheep alone He stands,
in desert air familiar land,
tears of blood seed the earth,
shouldered agony will bear its fruit.

The Mount of Olives a night of dread,
lovers whisper *Song of Songs*,
grace disrobes the Prince of Peace,
and clothes Him in Humanity's sin.

Illumined gaze in dark of night,
the cup of blood poured to brim,
a sip of death His will be done,
from reddened lips red roses bud.

# At home in me

*Lisa Bahlinger*

How could I not love you
though of course I got it
all wrong—how amazing to me you did not
leave, could come to make
your home with me—which I wonder at
twenty times a day, dazzled
by your coat on its peg, shoes by the fire,
an open book, plate and cup before you, while outside
a flock of spinning black birds fall in broken
wheels through the endless sky

where I cannot breathe, where
emptiness swallows me—

what a night with the sky falling
in great gray sheets
to slash down the slope of earth,
and those birds, where do they go, is there
a secret hiding place for them.

# Today

*Melanie J. Taormina*

When you have survived
the thing you thought you could never survive
and, so soon after,
survived the other impossible thing,
then, in short time
again, awakened to a stranger
(yourself) in your bed, you
learn to love better:  the sky
when it unfurls its blue and blares
its all-reaching, unapologetic light
like there's no tomorrow, but
there is a tomorrow, and it becomes
today, and you love better the smell
of washed sheets, of the eucalyptus Christmases
of childhood, of milk, cold and white,
in a simple, thick glass—
love better the breath in your nostrils
and the lungs that hold it, exchange it,
let it go.  You love, you see, better
all that you see because
you have survived — like the world
that doesn't turn in on itself
when winter creeps in, but stands
bare in face of the chill wind, limbs
out-reaching, sure, perfectly sure
more than frost will follow fall.

# A LOVE SONG TO MY MANIA

*Elise Seyfried*

Radiantly hopeless
Frozen solid and consumed
Clearheaded to distraction with
A truly false impression of what's real
How else can I explain the way I feel?
Beautifully misguided
Built of shards of broken glass
Just perfectly imperfect as
I'm laughing tears of sadness and delight
How else can I confess it's not all right?
Just slowly run
I'll wildly stand
You hold my mixed emotions in your hand
Just go to me
I'll come from you
We'll see what kind of damage we can do
Wonderfully wicked
Calm as corpses, full of pain
Alive as I have never ever been
How can I thank you, lover, as we part?
You made confetti from my armored heart

# THIS NIGHT
*Christmas, 2006*

*Melissa A. Chappell*


This night, our world is fed on violence
a nightmare birthed by the unholy communion
of terror and fear; this night, death holds dominion,
raining upon the innocents its terrible silence.

This night, our world dreams the dream
of the prodigal, who in some foreign land
dreams of home and a father's hand
embracing, consoling, even when it seemed

that all should not be well, that we might have remained
in the sty, staring at the trough of food,
breathing the dirty air, the stench so foul and rude;
an unholy communion of fear and shame.

This night, God dreams of the prodigal world.
There may be bombs and bullets that fly by night;
there may be the bloodied cloths of a child in the camera's sight,
but there was also once a babe in his mother's arms, curled,

crying in the darkness at an old, disheveled trough,
breathing in the mammal smells of ox and lamb and calf;
poor shepherds wandering from the fields, still with staffs
in hand: the innocents gathered 'round, hearts suddenly aloft.

This night, the sky was ablaze with the brush
of angel wings against all this aching earth.
Then let there fall over the world a holy, pregnant hush,
awaiting peace—that it may hold dominion, with the advent
    of this birth.

# THE SILVER DOLLAR CAFÉ
(Dedicated to Richard Sundgren)

*June L. Mita*


A common haunt for the khaki man
The white, stuccoed building
Blinked – Rhinegold, Miller –
In blue and red neon.
I could never go in
When mother parked sideways
In the gravel lot.
The sterile white door would open,
A perfect black rectangle at war
With the 5:30 sun,
Trying to defeat
Late afternoon light
Only it wouldn't win just yet.
Mother would enter the angled night
Then snap it shut.
Behind the steering wheel I would sing
"AMERICA, AMERICA,
God shed his grace on flashing flags."
The white door would blackly yawn again,
Spitting out Mother like a loose tooth
While Father leaned in a Lombardy sway.
It always looked like he was wearing
The Miller sign.
A bloody red 'M' trickled from his nose,
Writing out 'ILLER'
In melting grape lollipop lines
Down his khaki work shirt.

# DILEMMA

*Janet Rowse*

Inside church door farmers talk rain
Their buzz flows and blends with noisy children.
The last person shuffles down the aisle
Hesitating at mid pew,
Bowed heads sneak a glance.
Who could this laggard be?
Back pews full, squeezed bodies in regular places.
A farmer says
His own private prayer.
"For HE who knows
bring rain to my parched fields."

Ironic fate!

In front another farmer prays
An opposite prayer to HIM who knows.
"No rain to my uncombined fields—
Oh may He show His love to me!"

# MEDITATION ON GOOD FRIDAY

*Gregory Holmes Singleton*

This mocked cross mocks,
And He who is mocked
Mocks those who are mocking,
As did His mother
Who saw the poor fed,
The proud cast away.
And the poor become proud
And the proud become needy.

Mocking is mocked,
And destruction creates,
And renewed creation stops the cycle.
Mocking and mocked are made one;
Our salvation secured
On that throne of raw wood
Endured,
Then transcended.
And all is made new,
Eternally new,
With blood that pours
His life into ours.

# If The God Of Job

*Elizabeth Musselman*

If the God of Job
were to gird His Holy loins
and bellow
like a man, like a god—

And if these girded Holy loins
were to cry *mercy, mercy*
and lament
in this world, in this hour—

And if these howling Holy loins
were to enfold themselves
and break
with the assailed, with the betrayed—

And if these shattered Holy loins
were to tremble in the sun
and arise
ever near, ever strong—

Would the contours
of shrouded human frailty
suddenly
slowly
bind all things,
believe all things,
bear all things?

# PSALM 51

*Ann L. Hochscheid*

A pair of small bottles sits on my shelf.
    How long will they collect dust?
One is capped and sealed.
    Shall I save this treat for a lonely night?
The second is empty and the cap is gone
    But it is filled with memories.
I'll keep these tiny bottles
    And savor what is and is not within.
Cognac is not a solitary drink.
    It is best with old friends.

# Waiting Room

*Jerry Smith*

They come out, stand near me.
He gets her coat, holds it out,

she slips it on. He puts on his coat,
sees a package on the chair next to me.

Is this yours, dear?
I don't want to make off with this gentleman's

package. Looking up from my book,
I smile and say, I'd let you know.

Adjusting his scarf, he says to me,
I've already spent too much of my life in jail.

You should explain, his wife says.
They were all happy to see me, he says.

I could go there now and many would know me,
be happy to see me. He was a bail bondsman, she says.

What if they met you in a dark alley? I ask.
Most are not that bad, he says.

They get into trouble,
can't find their way out.

But I have, he says,
with a wink.

I've been paroled
into my wife's custody.

# I THINK OF YOU

*Fred Ise*

I think of you when evening's gentle shadows
lay down upon the streams and peaceful land,
when sun's last rays still touch the streams and meadows,
when night and day are walking hand in hand.

I think of you when stars adorn the heaven,
when moonlight shines through slowly sailing clouds,
when far away a clock does strike eleven,
when night's embrace our dreams and sorrows shrouds.

And still, at dawn, in morning's early hours,
when sun's first rays shine on a lonely hill,
when dew drops rest upon the sleeping flowers,
I think of you, my love, and always will.

# Walls

*Theresa M. Rochford*

*Some walls are easy to see*
concrete blocks of
gray-white cement
separating peoples,
sentinels of fear

*Some walls hide from us*
those that encase our lives
when we're not looking
and reaching out
becomes too hard

*Some walls remember*
displays of names
touched with tears
drawing people together,
shown to children

*Some walls are easy to see*
schoolyard walls
chalked with games
jumping with life,
sentries of hope

# FREE WILL

*Thomas J. Gilday*

When God allowed that ugly blight, you know within your heart
He never wanted greed and spite to play so large a part
Weakly with a quaking voice, the message rings with clarity
All of mankind has the choice to offer hate or charity
The future of this land is sealed, though hungry children pray
The people's crops are in the field and rotting day by day
There was food enough to ship for sale, and to keep the gentry fed
While at home the homeless wail, to morn their heaps of dead
Conquest has its price to pay you see, in men and means and
    mammon
Pitifully I say, God allowed the blight to be, but 'twas man that
    caused the famine...

# GRAPEVINE GEMS

*Arlene Johnson Jens*

In September, I hold a ritual
at the grapevine
and marvel at its annual prolificity,
its faithfulness to intertwine
production with tastefulness.

I lift the leaves as if opening
into the mysterious,
a treasure chest of jewels,
hastening a palate of delirious
sampling and uncertain wastefulness.

There they are.  Round purples,
perchance akin to rubies' fires.
In clusters of packed triangles,
they could be amethysts or sapphires:
God's architectural perfection.

I twist off a grape, settle it
where I can taste the gem.
What succulence!  Ripened grapes.
They deserve a diadem
as model for confection.

At the table of the Lord, I'll sup
and think of how mystical
is Jesus' cup.

# ASHES! ASHES!
Shrove Tuesday, 2006 –
*IN MEMORIAM* Cynthia Quere Camphouse (1962-1998)

*Ralph W. Quere*


I felt more ashen than shriven today,
No Mardi Gras on this end of "Old Man River!"
In morning prayers I wept for Krista and for Cyndie—
The juxtaposition too much!  I remember that
"Ring around the Rosey" (Iowa edition) ended threateningly:
"Ashes! Ashes! We all fall down!"  The primal fall
Brought death from sin on all!  That souls' cancer
Claimed us all—some, like Jesus and Cyndie, far too soon!

"You are dust and to dust you shall return!"
Ash Wednesday's good news?  Not exactly.
Nor is: "Prepare to meet your God!"
How about: "Repent!" Yes! To turn from flight
And fear of death to life-with-death-already-dead,
For eternal Easter lies beyond the ashes of Lent's end!

# MY 'LORD'S PRAYER'

*AnnJeanette Lee*

Our Father Who art in Heaven,
Hallowed be..(did I turn the oven on?)
Thy kingdom..(the roast won't get done for dinner.)
Thy will be do—..(I better call the kids.)
On earth as (what should I give him for his birthday?)
Give us this day our daily bread..(wow, where was my mind!)
And forgive us our trespasses as we forgive those who
    trespass against
Us. (I really mean it, Lord.)
For Thine is the kingdom, the power and the Glory
Forever and ever. (Please, God, help me concentrate.)
Amen

# The Farmer

*Sandee Gertz Umbach*

Ralph took the Amish farmer out through the fields
into the rye, the beans, the strangle of tall green corn,
stopped in the dead center and pulled up a fistful of dark brown soil.
"You know I need to sell this land, I'm too old for plowing
and it's either you or lots divided up,"
he told the man who'd been leasing his fields,
looking down into his wide-brimmed hat
his hands a deep brown outline against a white stiff shirt.

First summer sun pressed down, bleaching the top
of Ralph's gray-sheen hair while black crows counted
the seconds before the Amish man shifted
his feet, explained in measured tones
about his wife 20 miles down the road,
the elders who'd never allow him to own those acres, the rows
of straw-colored life popping beneath the cobalt sky.

Ralph had his hopes, watching him arrive each morning
to clang the barn bell, the steady way he led the Appaloosa
through his paces, the daily habits
he'd observed from his modular home
yards away from the barbed wire fence.
All that last year spent balancing
bills at the formica table, tucking
land offers into the family Bible, staring

out through the kitchen's café curtains,
to the Amish man's shadow
and the plump cows lazing
along the potholed road.

# GWENDOLYN BROOKS AT THE PODIUM

*Dwayne P. Daehler*

Rivulets of her imagination carve their meandering way
through the earth of her experience
shaping its landscape into the benediction of a story.
Syllables gathered at the headwaters of her heart
flow forth in a spring of clear words
open to reflection.

Her voice, now swelling, now plunging,
now rushing, now pooling,
carries a ceaseless stream of praises and laments.
Images overflow the banks of their poetry,
spilling into aside remarks—
all one great river form Black Grandmother Soul.
I am baptized in her deeps,
in her sacrament of wounded, weathered wisdom.

# What Matters

*Marilyn Peretti*

I try to remember what it was like
those few days after the smokey Towers fell,
when we peaceworkers saw:
Muslims vs. us, and we called each other

to the mosque in our suburbs,
gathering at the entrance on Sunday afternoon,
some men passing through our singing,
their scheduled prayers before them,

our worn-out peace songs all we had,
David strumming strings again,
old foolishness mixed with sincerity –
how much difference can it make?

White candles passed to all, short yellow flames,
and each uttering whatever words
could be found, when one could find them.
Maybe breathing in the direction of peace
is all that matters.

# Being HAD

*Brian Brown*

If we give a hug a day;
an acronym is born.
It comes the act of being HAD;
which can happen every morn'.
When coldness of the world enslaves
and bites in harsh retort;
We hug a day with all our might;
repealing feelings of every sort.
Rapture, tingle, warmth and ecstasy;
sensations living truth;
a hug a day in being HAD,
is nature's sweet Vermouth.
Be HAD today. Hug a day;
Don't pass it by; so sad;
Help someone know you care a lot
by giving them a HAD.

# CEILING STARS

*J. T. Haug*

On the drive home
all the lights blink yellow.
I notice how clear the stars seem,
unlike my thoughts.

My stomach feels
shallow.
I tell myself
it was that third beer,
or possibly the cigarette smoke,
but I already recognize
the taste of guilt
from making love to you.

Funny how the flesh
shields the spirit at times.
I tingled from your touch,
closed my eyes and fell inside
your crush.

Now, sinking into bed,
my spirit returns,
as it often does in the silence.
Only I'm not sure I like
what it has to say this time
as I sweat through morning,
watching my ceiling stars fade.

# Fish Tank

*Anne Basye*

For a few days the goldfish
looked sickly. His glowing fins
faded to white at the tips.
Suspicious foam gathered
on the surface. His laps
were listless.

I lied, and said he'd surely improve.
It was a shock to find him lifeless.
I flushed him away before anyone noticed.

When young I wondered
why fish vanished, and where they went.
Truth broke in when my gourami died.
I was too old for pretend, I guess,
for instead of dissembling,
my mother dissected
the fish on the toilet,
death's riddle probed,
poked, and prodded.

Easier are life's gifts: the sparrow,
stunned and shivering,
we fed with a dropper and nestled
in a box of tissue.
In the morning I expected
a corpse, but when we lifted
the lid it flew out,
resurrected.

# MY SHADOW

*Nancy Lund*

My little shadow has grown up
and lost some charm with age.
A pal who once played
winsome tricks of hide-and-seek
now casts longer, darker impulses
over moon full nights
and sun-illumined days.

My older shadow takes on shapes
no mirror dare reveal,
from serpent fangs to rabbit ears
to tiger claws to crocodile tears
she alters, threatening those near me
with scalpel edge -
then luring with pillow down.
She pushes, leads, urges me to enter
her dark mystery.
Sometimes she even talks to me,
assuming brazen authority
that reason can't enlighten.

At times my shadow has been
more troubling than useful,
and I admit to the temptation
of cutting her off
or denying our entangled history.
But she's a deepening part of my self -
and as an amputee of shadow
I'd be way off balance, incomplete.

# Tempter

*Cara Bertron*

Give a sign, a kingdom
with naked women on all
the rooftops.  Throw yourself
down into these fleshy angels.
Change stones to bread for their mouths,
envy and greed to sloths
in their beds four-toed and slow.
Believe, for it is foretold: the elect
at table, stuffed, toying with
idolatry intricate
and heavy to hold,
nestled in palm, heart –
believe, and remember the snake
coiled in your own belly, that want,
forty-day hunger,
what you, alone, need to survive
and what you think
you need – pride, promises,
the delicious wound of fang.

# With Love to Kevin

*Dorothea H. Pletta*

Life is: A twirling Frisbee
       A lob over the net
       A rebound shot into the basket
       Giggling girls
       The rat-a-tat-tat of the drums
Death is:  A rainy night; a slight skid on the road
Life is: A black and white bug; driving – top down
       Surrounded by music
       Hair tossing in the wind
       Aqua and white striped shirt and cap
Death is:  A rainy night; a slight skid on the road
       The early morning shrill ring of the phone
Life is:    The last day of school; end of another chapter
       A blue cap and gown; a gold rope of honor
       A fun weck at the beach
Death is:  A rainy night; a slight skid on the road
       The early morning shrill ring of the phone
       The grim reality of a hospital room
Life is: The loving memory of an impish smile
       A tousled head; long, long legs
       Fingers drumming on the table
Death is:  A rainy night; a slight skid on the road
       The early morning shrill of the phone
       The grim reality of a hospital room
       A cold, cold hard stone
But:     **Because He lives**
Life is: Eternal, Victorious
       Outside the mind and body; beyond space and time
**BECAUSE HE LIVES**
       Death has no power
       Death is no more

# WE CELEBRATE CHRISTMAS TOGETHER

*Grant Perry*

No one really knows
the month and the day,
or even the year, for that matter,
when Jesus was actually born;
but we have celebrated
December 25th so long
that if by some miracle
the actual date were discovered
to have been in August, say,
or October,
there would still be many
who would want to celebrate
on the good old date,
December 25th,
just as we always had;
and we might end up
having two Christmases,
as for years we had two Thanksgivings;
or families and churches might split on the issue,
just as my family has split
on the date when the world began.
I have a daughter
who does not believe in dinosaurs,
because that would make the world
older than the Bible says it is.
Don't argue with me about it.
I have learned not to argue with her.
I think she's wrong about her politics, too –
but she's my daughter and I love her,
and we celebrate Christmas together.

# You Are Supposed To Be Dying

*Deb Kosmer*

But you're not… not quickly

Anyways and days drag on and on

And I am caught in time waiting for

the inevitable but not knowing

when it will come and take you

from me and yet our life is

already over, the who we were is

gone and who we are now is just a

ghost of our past getting in the way

of today and my figuring out my

tomorrows alone without you.

# SIN

*Lynn Bonenberger*


Burgundy Scrabble board, tossed in the air
ivory lettered tiles scattered around the floor
half finished jumbo crossword done in pen
and the remaining answers don't fit in
an impossible sudoku of diagnoses from the DSM IV.


Is there a word?
There are no words.
There will never be a single word
for what is wrong with me
and why it is that I won't let You in.
No entrance, no language, no access
to my topsy-turvy
Alice in Wonderland
down is up and up is down world.
And why One might want entrance
to this realm when all I want is to exit it
for this, for sure
there is no word,
no answer.


I imitate, pretend, embellish circumstance
Suspicious I test why You would come close.
I push away, You can't come in.
Yet stubbornly I continue to take the broken pieces
and shove them back into a ragged hole
that doesn't fit but You.

# Love Overflowing

*Victor Pera*

On some lost mountain height obscure
a spring gives birth to flowing stream.
Soon other trickling riv'lets pure
unite in splashing sunlight's gleam.

A river moves in ceaseless flow,
its banks in lush green garments clad;
cascading, rushing, tumbling, now
its murmuring music makes hearts glad.

The waters spread and life they give
to frogs and fish and such as they.
Unnumbered beasts their thirst relieve;
there creatures myriad live their day.

From heaven above one starry night
love downward flowed in earth-bound stream,
and shepherds wondered at the sight
of infant laid in manger mean.

Life-giving river of endless grace,
that touches hearts, and flowers unfold
in color riot – in smiling face,
a shelter from earth's loveless cold.

The torrent sweeps in welling flood
as love gives birth to love, inside
the spirit born with new life-blood
spreads caring touch in growing tide.

# Bedtime Musing

*Roberta C. Stewart*

None of us can know the hour of passing.
It may steal upon us as a midnight prowler
who cowardly advances in shadows
around latticed vines to the back door
hidden from common view and
unguarded by the dog.
Even if we listen closely we will not
hear its step, the crushing of a leaf,
the scrape of a boot, heavy, across a
stone threshold. Only drifting off
will we look back and say, quietly,
*Oh, yes, it was you coming, after all.*
And we'll sigh that we had not
given our finer things to safekeeping:
a vase from Grandma
her silver spoon
albums bound with threads of gold
our gentle touch, accepting smile
our emptied hearts.

# EVE'S DAUGHTER

*Diane E. Tremper*

Bloodlines diverging

from Crescent's fertile land

to pulse thru Africa's rhythmic veins

and North to climes unthinkable

till forced South

they shudder

then slither down mountain coasts

to become Native peoples of straight black hair.

Then Africa's shores

are raped of blood and muscle

to toil in the new found land

where west pushed east

and blood lines converged

and hearts beat together with distant drums

to pulse weathered, but true,

once again.

# Live at Ten

*Kimberly Stenerson*

Leopards brag their speed and spots. Alligators
smile before the disemboweling. Lions roar their
death chant. Even roaches clatter, disgust, disquiet.
Murders infatuate us. Who? Why? Their
names in infamy titillate. But the victims
resound as wounds: "27 stab wounds,"
"shot 15 times," "Raped and strangled." One
of twelve, twenty, one hundred killed, unnamed.
A statistic, gore on speed, the waves of the TV's
roar. Anchorwoman smiles before the disemboweling.

# Sumatra Sultry Morning Sounds

*Jerry L. Schmalenberger*

While the thick night still blankets black
A proud rooster crows out his proleptic convoke.

Soon before daybreak has its predictable way
from minaret Muslim implores for Allah's prayers

Then Batak dogs begin their incessant barking
and diesel trucks belch black for day's transport

Palm fronds applaud the daylight's steamy emergence
Now moil of rattle trap becak starting their rounds

Full light moves in, black and white bird sings joy
for the start of another equatorial island day

Bath water poured over golden skinned bodies
splatter on moldy blue sweating tile floors

A loud speaker bellows Nommensen exercise instruction
Cucu Santi seeks her old white skinned Ompung

Rain on rusty tin roof drums out the island cacophony
of morning's Sumatra's sultry sounds.

# CHRISTMAS CHORALE AT TRINITY LUTHERAN

*Jane Piirto*

In October a green postcard arrives with a schedule of rehearsals.
People who don't sing all year—homemakers, city officials,
Bankers, doctors, accountants, clerks, teachers, secretaries, lawyers—
show up for this ritual, 60 voices, an orchestra of 25.

Each year the songs are the same—"Silent Night," "Hark the Herald
    Angels,"
"Joy to the World"; "Mary's Babe"; "African Christmas Chant"; "Oh Little
Town of Bethlehem"—in slightly different arrangements, depending on the
arranger. Some members borrow a CD so they can practice more.

Ron: "No, try just the first tenors." "Let's begin at measure 46."
His baton raps on the metal stand. We try not to whisper or side chat.
"Will you play that again for the second sopranos?" He asks Mark.
"Do it with the orchestra now! "Punch those notes." "Say 'Egg Shell Sees.'"

6 weeks of 3 rehearsals each; by the second Saturday in December
we are ready. Final run through rehearsal at 3:30. supper in the church
    basement,
sandwiches, soup, redgreen cookies. Then the 6:30 Saturday service (the
    casual one where they wear jeans and sing Bible camp choruses).
    Back at 8:30 Sunday.

Thus begins the season for parishioner and locals who pack all 3
    services.
We stand and sit on wide risers clad in white polyester robes with red
    trim, in the
big hall, Jack's Place. We are all together at last.
We are singing and it is holy.

Suddenly, down the dark center aisle comes the divine surprise.
Three five year old girl dancers, floating to "I Saw Three Ships Come
    Sailing In."
Each girl stretches a triangular sail, each is tiny, clad in a black leotard.
Tears sprout from our eyes and roll down our cheeks. We can hardly sing.

"On Christmas day in the morning"

# Ranger County West Virginia

*David Webb*

1.
Baptized in the rivers/buried in the hills.
Baptized in the rivers/buried in the hills.

When it rains in Ranger the hills give up their ghosts,
the mountains go for a walk.
When it rains in Ranger, the clay roads run all the way,
all the way to the valley below.

2.
Driving through the hills on Highway 77 into WV,
my grandfather's graves call out from the red clay gullies.

Driving through the hills where I was born
Nothing but silent/green/stone/dreams/

frog's waiting, only sitting.

# THE LEGACY OF A FARMER'S WIFE
*The fear of the LORD is the beginning of wisdom. Psalm 111:10*

*Roberta Meyer*


Wisdom comes from fearing God,
Respecting God,
Acknowledging God's omnipotent power.
Who better than a farmer's wife does this?
Her life depends on God's blessings.
Everyday she thanks God for her bounty
And everyday she hopes expectantly
For God's grace to provide.
During storms she looks forward to God's mercy
Realizing there are times she can do nothing
To change the lot given to her each day.
Hers is the challenge of creativity,
Using her resources to enable God's Love to shine.
In her faithfulness, her quiet witness
Speaks resounding to those in her nurturing care.
And as the last petal falls from her earthly existence,
The seeds she has sown will bloom for generations.

In Memory of Rose Meyer
        1920-2006

# GRACE

*Mary Hills Kuck*

Three small pots perched on my sill,
a daughter's gift to ease
long months of winter's gloom.

Narcissus sprang right up,
extended emerald stalks,
fanned its waxy bride-white blooms,
scent not innocent nor sweet.

Amaryllis raised a thumb,
slowly issued chartreuse leaves
as counterpoise for swan-necked stamen's
bud that blushed and split and birthed
twin trumpets of scarlet passion.

The lily lingered.
I watered and watched,
impatient, dug the bulb.
Discovered roots, buried fast.
Blamed myself.

Today, two fragile tendrils
reach above pot's edge,
pledge reprieve.

# Water Chestnuts

*Garret Grev*

It's in the taste of the water chestnut.
The texture, as you slide it in your mouth
Off the fork.
How it crunches between your teeth,
And travels down your throat.
A food without a match.
Something unique, not appreciated by all.
The smallest part of the meal,
But if it were not there everything would be lacking.
And God is in the details.
It's finding someone that eats the fortune with
The cookie.
Swallowing it all, in hopes that the best
May come true, like a little prayer.
It's looking across the table and realizing
That it's already been answered.

# #2 LATER THAT NIGHT....

*Lois Reiner*

Later that night, leaving the place where your eyes
had not opened since noon, where your heart stopped beating
eight hours later, we drifted, still stunned, towards the home
you had left only four days before. Where you had been
happy, so happy, in its pleasant spaces with friends
come to share conversation, with children and family
and walks into town and around Becky's garden.
With living!

How did it happen? This end of together, the dreaded
transition to solo, in so short a time? Where would I
find you now? Pasted in albums? Lauded in newsprint?
Framed on the mantel? Or had you become that star
hooked to heaven, looking in at the highest den window
later that night? Where ARE you?

This is my problem. We'd talked about dying but seldom
of "what then". "Heaven's a city, perfected" you offered,
my biblical scholar. "A beach on the Gulf's aqua waters"
I countered. But here was the test. All at once you were gone,
really gone from my bed, from these colorful rooms and
all that you loved about being alive! And I could not fathom
"Hereafter."
    Or you as a spirit. Or youthful and strong again,
somehow in actual touch with the others....all the others who
went on before. All the "brothers" and you back together
with Christ in the flesh and your mentor Ellul.
    Dear Schatz,
send me a clue! I need to imagine more clearly the "what then",
for heaven had happened  so often already , with you here.
Stay with me somehow while I'm cheering up  widows and testing
new strengths on the children, our remarkable children, who
vowed to keep feeding your vision and brought out The Plan
- did you notice? - later that night..... The Plan you had penciled in
margins for someone to find?

# These Years

*Verna Summerville*

With skin now splotched and netted,
My years begin to show;
My eyes no longer what they were –
My hair's near white as snow.

My beauty's drawn inside now
A'waiting for the day
When Jesus calls me to come home
And fold this shroud away.

Until that time I'm busy
A'working for our Lord.
For beauty's known by action –
And that's how Christ's adored.

If others still see beauty,
I pray it's not my own;
But that my hands and voice and life
Are serving Christ alone.

# Reflections of Spring

*Lemae Higgs*

Five lonely geese drift slowly north,
The cold night wind brings puffs with warm hints of the sea.

Soon dawn light will bring
Migrating meadow larks in chorus vast,
Sparrows searching twigs for tangled nests,
The lambs and their dams,
Bleating in noisy chorus,
All tease the cold air with the promise of spring.

On Milfoss I walk under night's splendor arrayed.
Still feeling the chill icy puffs from the heart's black void,
Impatient for spring but growing, stirring within,
I wait God's light like mocking bird and dove, voice mute,
To welcome my personal dawn.

# WINTER FUNERAL, NORWAY

*Gracia Grindal*

The mist holds its breath against the light
Shining through the fog over the evergreens;
Black barren branches etched against the white
Frame the official sorrows of the scene:
The pastor walking in his long black cape
Leading the white casket through the snowy fields
Past rows of gravestones flaked with ashen caps
Followed by mourners suited up like shades.
A study in black and white, except the red
Roses, sprays of them, their petals fall
Glowing like blood on the white coffin lid,
Their passion incarnadines the mourning pall
Eden goes down in the dust the pastor throws,
Fresh dirt clattering onto the lawn of snows.

# THE POETS

**John Alexanderson** is a member of St. Paul's Lutheran Church in Doylestown, PA, is a Prudential retiree, school bus driver, and grandfather. He is thankful to still be a runner at age 61, and to have been published somewhat frequently. His first chapbook, *When Least Expected*, appeared in 2006. Proceeds have benefited Katrina rescue/recovery.

**Frank Attanasia** is a native of Brooklyn, New York, and has written poetry since the third grade. He is a Social Worker, working in Hospice Care, and is a rostered deacon of The Evangelical Lutheran Church in America – Metropolitan New York Synod. He is a father to his son, Matthew David, and his daughter Christina Ruth, and is a husband to his wife, Reverend Harriet Wieber. His work has been published in *Healing Ministry*, *The Poetry Church*, *Amaze-The Cinquain Journal*, and *The Adirondack Review*. Frank Attanasia currently serves Bethany Lutheran Church in Brooklyn, New York.

**Alice M. Azure** has had poems, short fiction and essays appear in *Eating Fire, Tasting Blood: An Anthology of the American Indian Holocaust*; *Shenandoah*; *The Cream City Review*; *Native Chicago*; and *Skins: Drumbeats from City Streets*. She recently retired from a long career in the United Way system, having administered program grants and community studies in such places as Rock Island, Illinois; Alexandria, Virginia; Green Bay, Wisconsin and Gales Ferry, Connecticut. In all those cities, she enjoyed powwow dancing, tribal social gatherings and many friendships. She is of Mi'kmaq, French and Norwegian ancestry.

**Lisa Bahlinger** holds a B.A. in English from Louisiana State University, and an M.F.A. in Writing from Vermont College. She worked as a freelance children's book editor for several years for

Boyds Mills Press, a Highlights for Children company; for Design Press at Savannah College of Art and Design. She also edited a collection of Lenten devotions as a youth resource for the ELCA world hunger initiative. Ms. Bahlinger lives in Memphis, Tennessee, with her husband and daughters, where she is a member of St. Luke Lutheran Church.

**Richard F. Bansemer**, Bishop Emeritus of the Virginia Synod, has served as a pastor and bishop of the Evangelical Lutheran Church in America since 1966. Now retired, he leads retreats on spirituality for clergy and laity and writes librettos for oratorios and other musical works. *Job the Oratorio* premiered in 2004, and *Mary the Mother of Jesus* premiered on May 22, 2006. Other works are in progress. The author of ten books, his most recent, *Getting Ready for the New Life*, was published in 2004 by Augsburg Fortress Publishing House. Richard is a graduate of Newberry College (1962) and Lutheran Theological Southern Seminary (1966), and holds honorary Doctor of Divinity Degrees from Roanoke College and Newberry College. He and his wife Mary Ann have three sons, John, Aaron, and Andrew, and four grandchildren, Katherine, Emily, Phillip and Micah.

**Anne Basye** is a member of Unity Lutheran Church in Chicago ad the author of *Sustaining Simplicity: A Journal*. She is now finishing the graduate creative writing degree she forgot to get in her 20s, at Northwestern University.

**Kera Béh** is a young author who loves God and the amazing feats He accomplishes in His creation. Her poems mainly focus on His power and how easy it really is to find beauty in things which are normally overlooked or unappreciated. She often feels quite insignificant in all the beauty around her, then remembers that God considers her (as well as the rest of mankind) the best part of what He made. Kera lives in Indiana, out in the country, where she can best observe God's wonders and glory. She published a book earlier this year entitled *The Six of Airys: First Quest*.

**David Rask Behling** was born in Rhode Island, but grew up all over the world, finally settling in Albert Lea, Minnesota. Currently, he teaches English, mainly Developmental Writing and First Year Composition at Waldorf College, in Forest City, Iowa (a college of the Evangelical Lutheran Church in America). Behling is married to an ELCA pastor, and they have three children. He has been writing non-fiction about
parenting and family, mainly for newspapers and magazines, since 1991, and started working on fiction writing as part of an MFA program he began in the summer of 2005.

**Kevin Bergeson** is a musician with three independently released albums of faith infused folk rock. His wanderings from Montana to Mississippi to Las Vegas flavor his suburban observations with Lutheran roots. He resides in Saint Paul, Minnesota with guitar in one hand, Bible in the other, and two feet ready for his first pastoral call.

**Cara Bertron** is a fifth-generation Texan who currently lives in California. She grew up amidst the barbeques and potlucks of a Lutheran church, explored Catholic and Episcopal rituals for many years, then fell in love with University Lutheran Church in Berkeley, where she now attends services. Cara works variously in historic preservation, nonprofits, and the warm kitchens of a bakery. She likes to write letters, play soccer, cycle, cook, and construct ambitious pipe dreams with friends and family.

**Ann Boaden** received her undergraduate degree in English from Augustana College, Rock Island, Illinois, and her master's and doctorate in English from the University of Chicago. She teaches literature, writing fiction, and creative nonfiction at Augustana. Her work has appeared in a variety of literary journals including *Big Muddy: a Journal of the Mississippi River Valley, Buffalo Carp, Knight Literary Journal, Outloud Anthology of Poetry, Northwoods Journal, The Heartlands Today, Wascana Review*, and in the anthology *Christmas on the Great Plains* published by the University of Iowa.

155

**Katie Bombardi** began life being knit together in her mother's womb. However, her desire for home has not kept her from wandering around aimlessly about the world.

**J.L. Bond** is a homemaker, late-bloomer poet, and artist who resides on the Canadian prairies. Her work has appeared in literary journals, church magazines, and local newspapers in Canada. St. Paul Lutheran is her church of choice; she is an adherent, and connects with the Lutheran faith tradition. However, she is not a member. Her faith journey has involved many "persuasions;" thus, she identifies herself less by denomination and more by relationship with Christ.

**Stephen Bond** is an ordained ELCA pastor serving two congregations in west-central Pennsylvania – New Life Lutheran Church in Marion Center, PA and Hope Lutheran Church in Homer City, PA. A 2006 graduate of Trinity Lutheran Seminary in Columbus, Ohio, he is new to pastoral ministry, but grew up in Lutheran congregations and was nurtured into faith within Lutheran thought, worship, and culture. His wife, Sarah, and he live in Indiana, PA. He is previously unpublished as a poet, but enjoys reading and writing poetry, song, and prose, preferably over a cup of black coffee.

**Lynn Bonenberger** is a student of poetry and is working to have her first poems published. She lives in Pittsburgh, PA where she works as the director of the senior center.

**Mark Bouzard** was born into a career military family. He has lived overseas and across the United States, but has spent the majority of his years in the Central Texas area. He has trained as a computer assisted designer, but his heart belongs to printmaking and graphic arts. "Two Sonnets For My Brother's Ordination" is his first poem to be published.

**Jan Bowman** is Emerita Professor of English at California Lutheran University where she has taught courses in English, Women's Studies, and Religion since 1974. Her life in the church began in a Swedish Lutheran parish in Illinois and grew from that small ethnic circle to embrace the world as her place of belonging, and its religions as expressions of faithfulness worthy of study and respect. She has published work on a variety of subjects, and her poems have appeared in *The Cresset* and in *Weavings: A Journal of the Christian Spiritual Life*. In 2005 *Carved Like Runes*, a collection of her poems, was published by Lutheran University Press, a division of Kirk House Publishers.

**David Brauer-Rieke** was born in Seattle, WA on November 3, 1955 and graduated from Pacific Lutheran University in 1978 with a B.A. in Economics. In 1982 he graduated from Luther Northwestern Theological Seminaries with an M.Div. His wife, Gretchen, is also a PLU graduate with a Masters Degree in Nursing from the University of Minnesota and certification as a Nurse Midwife. They have three children, Aaron, Clare, and Nate. An ELCA pastor of 19 years, his current call to Atonement Lutheran Church began in January of 2005. Prior to this he served 18 years as pastor of Christ the King Lutheran Church in Milton-Freewater, OR (1987-2004).

**Brian L. Brown** is a native of a Wisconsin dairy farm, but now lives near Madison with his wife (Mary) and their Maltese dog (TC). The Browns have a son (Andrew) and daughter (Kimberly). Brown has worked in the information technology sector of the insurance industry for over 34 years. He graduated from Oregon High School in Oregon, WI and has a two-year associate's degree in Police Science. He enjoys creative writing, motorcycling, sport shooting and most of all, spending time loving his family.

**Melissa Chappell** is a native of Pomaria, South Carolina. She attended Newberry College and graduated with a degree in Music Theory as well as a minor in Religion. After college, she earned the Master of Divinity degree from Lutheran Theological Southern Seminary in Columbia, South Carolina. Her first call was to St. James Lutheran Church in Chilhowie, Virginia. After six years there, she served as interim pastor at St. John Lutheran Church in Abingdon, Virginia. Currently she is on medical disability, but remains active through writing, advocating for various causes, attending retreats, and spending time with her dog Liam. She has self-published two volumes of poetry: A *Lesser Light* and *The Turning*. Her work has also appeared in *The Clinch Valley Review*.

**Dale P. Chesley** has been a Lutheran pastor for 30 years. Born and raised in Iowa, he has served parishes in North Dakota, Iowa and presently at Good Shepherd Lutheran Church in Ashland, Wisconsin.

**Constance E. Ciway** grew up in Roselle, Illinois, and graduated from Carthage College in Kenosha, Wisconsin with bachelor's degrees in Fine Art and Graphic Design. She also studied creative writing and Spanish. She has written poetry since she was in middle school, and has had a personal relationship with Christ since she was nineteen. She loves poetry because it is an intimate way of looking at a single shard of life. The work she does is the exploitation of the simple, mundane of life and illustration of the beauty and pain of the everyday. She believes that it is the privilege of the artist believer to use his or her craft to show the world God himself.

**Le Anne Clausen** spent four years as a human rights worker in Israel, Palestine, Iraq and several other locations. She is a nationally prominent human rights activist, public speaker, and author, and has published work in *The Lutheran magazine*, and numerous seminary student newspapers and internet sites. Clausen is a M.Div. student at Chicago Theological Seminary, with a previous MA in Christian-Muslim relations. She recently founded the ecumenical Seminary Student Action Network, and is editing her first book about her experiences in the Middle East.

**Robert Cording** teaches English and creative writing at College of the Holy Cross where he is the Barrett Professor of Creative Writing. He has published five collections of poems: *Life-list,* which won the Ohio State University Press/Journal award, in 1987; *What Binds Us To This World*; *Heavy Grace*; *Against Consolation*; and most recently, *Common Life*. He has received two grants in poetry from the National Endowment of the Arts and two from the Connecticut Commission of the Arts. In 1992, he was poet-in-residence at the

Frost Place in Franconia, New Hampshire. His poems have appeared in the *Nation, Image, AGNI, Georgia Review, Kenyon Review, New England Review, Poetry, DoubleTake, Orion, Paris Review, New Yorker* and many other magazines. He lives in Woodstock, Connecticut with his wife and three children.

**Karen Cornish** is a middle-aged, life-long Lutheran, who has studied for a career in English Education but spent her life in food service at a hospital in Davenport, Iowa. She loves to read and enjoys poetry very much. She has had several poems printed in the *Quad-City Times*, two published in *Mimesis* (a book that Marycrest College did at one time, several published in *Dynamis* (a newsletter for college students that a pastor created) and one selected for publication by the *Delta Epsilon Sigma honor society*, of which she was a member.

**Barbara Crooker** has published poems in magazines such as *Tiferet, The Christian Science Monitor, The Christian Century, Christianity and Literature, Sojourners, Windhover, Perspectives, Literature and Belief, America, Rock and Sling, Radix, Relief*, and *The Cresset*; anthologies, including *Good Poems for Hard Times* (Garrison Keillor, editor)(Viking Penguin), *Looking for God in All the Right Places* (Loyola Press), *Hunger Enough: Living Spiritually in a Consumer Soc*iety (Pudding House Publications), *Summer: A Spiritual Biography of the Season* and *Spring: A Spiritual Biography of the Season* (SkyLights Paths Publishers), and a full-length collection, *Radiance*, which won the 2005 Word Press First Book Award, and was a finalist for the 2006 Paterson Poetry Prize. In 2003, she received the Thomas Merton Poetry of the Sacred Award (Stanley Kunitz, judge).

**Dwayne Daehler** is a resident of West Lafayette, Indiana, a sometime poet, a sometime photographer, a sometime traveler, and a full-time ELCA interim pastor. He is married, and he and his wife, Marcia, enjoy outdoor activities like camping, hiking, and cross-country skiing. For five years (1998-2003) he took a break from parish ministry to serve as co-director of ARC Retreat Center near

Cambridge, Minnesota. Living in a log house tucked in the woods along the Rum River, he had a perfect setting to indulge his love of photography and writing. His poetry has been published in a chapbook anthology, *Granville Poets*.

**Tiffany Demke** received her B.A. from Saint Louis University, M.A. from Concordia Seminary St. Louis, Th.M from the Lutheran School of Theology and is currently pursuing a M.Div. at Catholic Theological Union and a Ph.D. at the Lutheran School of Theology. Tiffany's academic interests include contemplative studies, neurotheology, whiteheadian metaphysics and Franciscan spirituality.

**Ann Dixon** has had her poetry published in the journal *ICE-FLOE: International Poetry of the Far North*. Her poems for children have appeared in the magazines *Cricket* and *Ladybug*, as well as the anthology *Once Upon Ice and Other Frozen Poems*. In addition, she has authored numerous essays and magazine articles, several of which have appeared in *The Lutheran*, and has written eight children's books. Ann Dixon is a born-and-raised, though occasionally strayed, Lutheran, and is currently a member of Good Shepherd Lutheran Church in Wasilla, Alaska.

**Barbara Focht Dorgan** hails from Reading, PA, but has resided in Montgomery, AL for the past 24 years, where she is a member of Messiah Lutheran Church. She has two grown children and three grandchildren. In past years Mrs. Dorgan has traveled extensively throughout Europe due to her own employment in Germany with the U.S. government (1958), and again in Munich, Germany (1978-83) with her husband and children, due to her husband's work. She enjoys reading, writing, travel, art, and music. Her poetry has previously been published in three different college literary magazines, and her work has appeared in the *World of Poetry* anthology (March 1988 – Sacramento, CA), in which she was awarded an Honorable Mention for her poem, "Sometime in November."

**Anders Dovre** has been previously published in *Sequel* and has been a finalist in a National Federation of State Poet Societies competition. He is a senior English major at Simpson College in Indianola, Iowa.

**Helen Eikamp** and Fred celebrated their 60th wedding anniversary May 8, 2006. They have three sons, Kevin married to Rita lives in Iowa; Rod married to Cindy lives in Aberdeen SD, Curtis married to Jeanine lives in Wisconsin. They have five grandkids (Emily, Adam and Peter) and five great grandkids (Ike, Leo, Max, Elsa and Miles). Helen graduated from Britton High School and attended USD of Vermillion for a year. She is member of First Lutheran Church and American Legion Auxiliary in Britton. She has eleven books in print, including *Fact 'n Fancy*, published by Tesseract Publications. Most are collections of her poetry and program material. The next book will involve the lives of two cousins, in their own words.

**Brad Froslee** is an ordained Lutheran pastor serving St. Luke Presbyterian Church, Minnetonka, MN. Brad received his M.Div. from Harvard Divinity School in Cambridge, MA, after having received his B.A. from St. Olaf College in Northfield, MN. Brad's poetry reflects a celebration of small-town life, having grown up in Vining, Minnesota, as well as the urban life and diverse backgrounds he has experienced as a pastor. Brad has worked with First Lutheran Church, Lynn, MA, Resurrection Lutheran, Oakland, CA, and Lutheran students at Boston University. Alongside writing, Brad has been involved in community organizing, working on issues facing refugees, addressing the issue of sexuality in congregations, and involvement with Latin America, Haiti, and the Pine Ridge Indian Reservation.

**David M. Frye** and his wife, Anne, live with their two Labradoodles, Sam and Zeke, in Denton, near Lincoln, Neb. David's son, Benjamin, is a music performance major at Bethany College, and Anne's daughter, Tara, is attending medical school at Oregon Health & Science University in Portland. David is a Pennsylvania native who moved to Nebraska and was ordained in 1989. He has served congregations in Potter, Gurley, and York, Neb., and worked as a hospice chaplain. In his free time, he enjoys photography, poetry, pottery,

T'ai Chi, comic books and travel. Ann and David are members of Shepherd of the Hills Lutheran Church, Hickman, Neb.

**Thomas J. Gilday** published a book of poems entitled *Violets in the Grass* (Mastof Press) in June of 2004. That same year he published a book of short stories entitled *I Don't Know, I Was Just a Kid*. This book recalled memories of growing up poor in a big city. Thomas is a retired firefighter from Philadelphia. He and his wife, along with their children and grandchildren, are members of St. Paul Lutheran Church in Millersville, PA. His wife sings in the choir and he has taught Adult Bible classes and is currently serving on church council.

**Susan D. Gordon**, a retired teacher from Batavia, IL, is now a member of Good Shepherd Lutheran Church in Lena, IL. She and her husband Virgil live with son Tim in Orangeville, IL where they raise registered Scottish Highland cattle. Susan also has four other children, Andrew, David, Tim, (Arizona) and Meghan (Sycamore, IL). She enjoys sharing her writing and says her words are "sent from a gracious God."

**Melinda Graham**, a poet and nurse, lives in rural Saline County Kansas. Some of her published work has appeared in *PlainSpoken: Chosen words, Chosen lives* (Weary Women Press) a collection by six Kansas poets, and *Whispers in the Wind,* a chapbook. Selected work was adapted and performed as reader's theater at McPherson College. She has been the recipient of three artist's grants from Salina Arts and Humanities, a group grant from Kansas Arts and Humanities and is currently doing grant work creating a body of poems and linked stories inspired by her vocation in the art of nursing. Mindy is also a wife, mother and grandmother and lives and worships in Falun/Salemsborg Lutheran Parish near Smolan, Kansas.

**Garret Grev** was raised in the Brainerd Lakes area of Minnesota. There he grew up sandwiched between Rock Lake and the Pillsbury State Forest with his brother, Ethan, and parents, Paul and Jean. Garret is a recent graduate of Luther College in Decorah, Iowa, where he earned degrees in English, Spanish, and Economics and was a member of the Luther Norse Football team. He currently lives in Spicer, MN, where he spends time reading, writing, enjoying the outdoors and nothing in particular, when not at work for Target Corporation.

**Gracia Grindal**, a graduate of Augsburg College, received an M.A. from Luther Seminary and an M.F.A. in poetry from the University of Arkansas. She joined the Luther Seminary faculty as associate professor of pastoral theology and ministry, communications in 1984, and was named professor of rhetoric in 1992. Grindal came to the seminary from Luther College, Decorah, Iowa, where she was a member of the English department faculty from 1968 to 1984. Her books include: *A Revelry of Harvest*; *Hymns Of Grace*; *We are one in Christ*; *Speaking of God*; *Scandinavian Folksongs*; *Singing the Story*; *Sketches Against the Dark*; and *Pulpit Rock*. She has published many articles on the history of Scandinavian-American Lutheran hymnody, and the women of the Norwegian-American Lutheran churches. In addition, her hymns and hymn translations are published in hymnals of several mainline churches.

**Amy Grogan** discovered her love of writing in high school. Even though she is an Electrical Engineer, she earned a master's degree in English (Creative Writing) from Wright State University, and gravitates toward creative endeavors. Most recently, she has written family devotionals, youth newsletters, songs, and her favorite, poetry. She has been published in the *Vincent Brothers Review*.

**Scott Hamre** is a life-long Lutheran married 25 years to his wife Carol. He was briefly a seminary student at Luther Northwestern in Saint Paul, and now is very fulfilled teaching young adults with severe handicapping conditions at a nearby public high school. A member of Faith Lutheran Church in Yucaipa, CA, Scott is Outreach chairperson, and his wife is church President. They both also either teach or help with Sunday school. They have one son, Nick, who is a freshmen at Sonoma State University in Rohnert Park, CA. They own and care for two dogs (Jack Russell, Daisy, rules the roost; Beagle, Bailey, does what she's told).

**Elayne Clipper Hanson** is a charter member of Writers at the Portage, and Pauquette Wordcrafters; a member of Wisconsin Fellowship of Poets and past president of Wisconsin Regional Writers, Inc. She has been published in many newspapers, magazines and anthologies: *Milwaukee Journal*, *Portage Daily Register*, *The Observer*, *Country Poet*, *FREE VERSE*, *WFOP Poetry Calendars* and anthologies, *The Viking*, *The Bond*, and many more. She was a columnist for ten years in three publications, has won the Golden Crow award seven times, first place Yarns of Yesteryear, has placed in Al P. Nelson, Florence Lindemann and Jade Ring contests of WRWA; has two books published, *So This is Me*, a chapbook of poetry and *The World According to Clipper*, a collection of her columns and poetry.

**Raymond Hartung** is a man of many years, and although a native of Minnesota, he and his wife moved to Arizona in 1991 for health reasons. He has three published books, the latest of which is a child's book, *Bugsy and the White Holstein*. His last novel is a mystery named *Venom*, which takes place in Tucson, Arizona. Raymond considers poetry to be the single most interesting avocation he works at.

**Jon T. Haug** is a seminarian enrolled in the Masters of Divinity program at Pacific Lutheran Theological Seminary in Berkeley, CA. Currently on internship at Luther Place Memorial Church in Washington, DC with his wife, he plans on taking the last year of his degree at the Lutheran Theological Seminary at Gettysburg. He defines himself as a storyteller both through his preaching and his poetry.

**Ned Hayes** is a frequently published writer whose poetry and theological ponderings have appeared in *The Mid-American Review*, *Seattle Theology Review*, *Amelia*, *Hot Ink*, and many other journals and magazines. His work has also been anthologized in *Divine Aporia: Postmodern Conversations About the Other*. Currently, Ned is a student at Luther Seminary in St. Paul, MN, but he claims Olympia, Washington as his home.

**Caleb Hendrickson** is a student at St. Olaf College in Northfield, Minnesota, and is studying studio art (printmaking, sculpture, and video) and religion. He has exhibited his visual art in school exhibitions at St. Olaf and at his high school, Minnehaha Academy. He also has been a part of exhibitions at Concordia College, St. Paul, and Outsiders and Others Gallery located in downtown Minneapolis. Caleb plans on pursuing a Master of Fine Art Degree or a Master of Divinity. He has been an active member in the ELCA community and the Lutheran tradition.

**Dennis Herschbach** is a licensed lay-minister serving Our Saviour's Lutheran Church, a small congregation found on the north shore of Lake Superior in Minnesota. He belongs to the League of Minnesota Poets, the Arrowhead Poets' Chapter, and has worked on a series of grief poems since the death of his wife in 2005. Among other verses he has written is a group of poems relating to the Boundary Waters Canoe Area Wilderness. He is new to poetry writing, but has been encouraged by friends and fellow writers.

**Caty Heyn** was baptized, raised and confirmed in the Lutheran tradition. There were times when she had more doubt than faith, but that changed her senior year in high school when she survived a rollover car accident in which she felt angel arms around her. Since then, she has graduated from California Lutheran University. Although hoping she would be published by the time she was thirty, she watched her thirty-third birthday come and go. However, soon after, she reaffirmed her commitment to 'take herself seriously' as a poet. The next day, her mother gave her a copy of her church's monthly newsletter, which happened to include the call for poetry to be published in SIMUL. She believes that was God's way of encouraging her.

**Lemae Higgs** is serving her fourth year in parish ministry at a wonderful small rural congregation – to be 140 years old this year! The congregation keeps her very busy and she is blessed by a wonderful call from God.

**Laura Hirneisen** lives on a farm in southeastern Pennsylvania. Her poetry and prose appears in or is forthcoming from *Blueline*, *2River View*, *400 Words*, *Monkeybicycle*, and other journals.

**Ann L. Hochscheid** received her BBA from the University of Cincinnati in 1953 and went on to become the Owner/Manager of a small chain of ready-to-wear stores in Kansas and Missouri. She is now retired. Ann is a member of Our Savior's Lutheran Church in Topeka, Kansas, and is active in the Topeka Civic Theatre, the Topeka Haiku Group, and the Topeka Lady Luck Investment Club. She serves as Branch Chair for both the American Association of University Women and the National League of American Pen Women. Ann has been a watercolorist for many years, and quilting has always been one of her joys. She began writing five years ago, and hopes that she never becomes too old to be creative.

**Linda Holmes** a city girl with a country heart, found her niche when she and her husband, David, moved to a small farm on 30 pine-studded acres in Aitkin County in 1991. She enjoys beekeeping, reading, writing, gardening, caring for a menagerie of chickens, ducks and 4 cats, and is never bored. Linda loves outdoor adventures and has tried her hand at wild ricing, making maple syrup, peeling pine logs and helping build her log cabin retreat on their land. Her nature essays have been published in *Lake Country Journal*, *Voices for the Land II*; and a poem in *Dust & Fire*. She and her husband are active members of First Lutheran Church, Aitkin, Minnesota and their community.

**Lois Batchelor Howard** is a graduate of The University of Michigan in Music. She has won dozens of local and national writing contests. Her poetry, short stories, and articles have been published in the *National League of American Pen Woman magazine* (and anthologies of winners in branch contests), *POET magazine*, *The Toledo Blade*, the *Santa fe Digest*, *Grandmother Earth*, *San Diego College CITY WORKS*, and other newspapers and literary journals. Music is her vocation and, between teaching and practicing and performing, the available time to write is brief, often just long enough for a poem "to write her!" She is the organist and music director at La Jolla Lutheran Church in La Jolla, CA, where she has served for eight fulfilling years.

**Chuck Huff** was born and raised in the Deep South and migrated to Minnesota where he is now is Professor of Psychology at St. Olaf College. There he teaches social psychology, ethics, and writing. He is currently doing empirical research on the moral psychology of computer professionals, having identified and interviewed moral exemplars in this profession.

**Eric Huff** was born and raised in Wheaton, Illinois, and attends St. Paul Lutheran Church. He is currently a student at Carthage College majoring in English, with a minor in both secondary education and creative writing. He is currently the vice president of the Poetry Underground and the secretary of the Gospel Messengers. In 2006 Eric received an honorable mention with the Chapin-Tague and Dr. Juanita Jones award in Poetry.

**John Hulteen** was born in 1916 in Clearbrook, MN, and in 2006 celebrated 65 years of marriage to his wife, Dorothy Busse. With their three children they raised and showed sheep at state and county fairs for several years. He was active in 4-H leadership and their Lutheran church, and has served as county assessor. This job eventually led him to Bismarck, ND where he served as State Supervisor of Assessments until his retirement in 1983. He now resides in Thief River Falls with his wife.

**Fred Ise** was born in Estonia in 1925 and came to this country in 1949 as a war refugee. After serving in the US Army during the Korean War, he traveled extensively around the world working for US defense programs. He settled in Maryland in 1972, where he was employed at the Goddard Space Flight Center. He retired in 1995 residing now with his wife Ann in Ellicott City, Maryland. Mr. Ise has written many poems in his native language of which a number have been published. In the last years he has written also in English.

**Alexander M. Jacobs** received his B.A. from Muhlenberg College in 1963, and went on to receive his M.Div. from the Lutheran Theological Seminary at Philadelphia in 1966. He has served as a parish pastor in Philadelphia, and as campus pastor at Wayne State University, Stanford University, and the University of Wisconsin, Milwaukee. He was the Director of Gamaliel Chair in Peace and Justice for 20 years, and for the last few years he has served in various Interim Ministries. Alexander Jacobs has published poems in *Sojourners*, *Lutheran Partners*, and *Campus Ministry Journal Meditations in The Word in Season.*

**Michael E. Jenkins** is originally from Nashville, TN; graduated from Middle Tennessee State University in 1978 and Lutheran Theological Southern Seminary in 1982. He was ordained in 1982 and served St. James Lutheran, Greeneville, TN and First Lutheran, Nashville, TN. In 1988 he entered the US Army as a chaplain and served in various locations both in the US and overseas. He retired in 2005 and is presently serving as pastor of Faith Lutheran, Clay, AL. He is married to Bonnie; they have two children: Christopher (20) and Rachael (18).

**Arlene Johnson Jens** was born in 1926 on a farm near Fairfield, Iowa. When she was 13, her first of many poems were published. She became a registered nurse with a specialty in caring for the elderly in nursing homes and presented seminars through Easter Iowa Community College. She's published articles in nursing and church periodicals; booklets of poetry and two books. She's listed in *The World Who's Who of Women* (1973-1976); *Dictionary of International Biography* (1973); and *Personalities of the West and Midwest* (1972). Arlene and her husband Wayne live in Davenport, Iowa, and are active in Grace Lutheran Church. The Jens' have two sons and six grandchildren.

**Christine Jensen** lives in Drayton, North Dakota, with her husband Tracy. She is on the board of directors of Abriendo Fronteras, "Opening Borders," a non-profit organization working to conduct travel delegations, create longstanding relationships, and increase awareness of issues surrounding life on the United States/Mexico border. The majority of her time is spent as a free-lance writer and guest speaker. She wrote her first poem when she was 7-years-old called "Jumping Frogs." Christine Jensen is a member of Skjeberg Lutheran Church of rural Drayton, North Dakota.

**Jeffrey Johannes** is a poet, artist, and teacher. His work has been published widely in journals including *English Journal, WI Poets' Calendars, Fox Cry Review, Modern Haiku, Acorn* and *Rosebud*. An award winner in both forms, he has won and/or placed in all categories of the WI Fellowship of Poets' (WFOP) Triad Contest. A member of WFOP, Riverwood Round Table, Midstate Poetry Towers, and The Entendres' (an on-line critique group), Jeffrey enjoys camaraderie with other creative folks. Listed on bookthatpoet.com, Jeffrey is a life-long Lutheran and member of First English Lutheran in WI Rapids, WI.

**Joan Wiese Johannes** has been publishing poetry for 25 years and writing music for the Native American Flute for 10. Winner of the Triad and Trophy Poem contests sponsored by Wisconsin Fellowship of Poets, and a finalist for The Muse Prize from WFOP and the John Lehman Award sponsored by the WI Academy of Science, Arts, and Letters, her poems have been published in numerous journals. She has also published two chapbooks, *Mother Less Child* and *Myopic Nerve*, as well as sheet music for *Native American* and a flute duet CD, *Hyoalinda*. The daughter of a Methodist minister, Joan joined First English Lutheran Church in WI Rapids, WI after her marriage to Jeffrey Johannes, also a poet. They live in Port Edwards, WI.

**Arnie Johanson** is Professor Emeritus of Philosophy at Minnesota State University, Moorhead. He currently resides and writes poetry in Durham, North Carolina. His poems have been published in *Light, Main Street Rag, Red Weather, Pinesongs,* and *Sincerely, Elvis*. He has won two prizes for formal poetry from the North Carolina Poetry Society.

**Linda M. Johnson** is a wife and mother and lives in the same town in northeastern Minnesota she grew up in. She believes in dreaming, the power of prayer, and the beauty of the written word. Ask for her advice and she'd say "if you love someone tell them so, offer your company coffee, and read poetry just for fun." Her previous publications include *Dust & Fire*, *The Finnish-American Reporter*, *The Moccasin*, *Otter Tail Review - Volume Two*, and *Nothing To Do With Camels*: a collaboration of poetry and short-stories through Beecroft Writer's Group. She has Radio credits through Savage Press, and in June of 2007 will be published in *Encore*: an annual anthology through the NFSPS.

**Katherine Kennon** is originally from Van Horne, Iowa. She is a student of English and Philosophy at Luther College and will graduate in 2008. Following graduation, it is her intention to enter a graduate program to study English literature. Throughout her life she hopes to be a widely published author of both poetry and fiction. Katherine Kennon and her family are members of Trinity Lutheran Church in Cedar Rapids, Iowa.

**Norma Thorstad Knapp**, Alexandria, MN, has had several poems, short stories, and essays published in various publications — locally, regionally, and nationally. Two of her stories have won awards: the Carol Bly Award in Nonfiction for her story in *Dust and Fire 2001* and a Top Ten Award for her story of fiction in *Lakes Alive*, the July/August 2003 issue. Norma's background includes nursing, education, and bereavement facilitation. Now retired, she concentrates on writing, hospice work, and playing with her four grandchildren. In 2002 she was awarded an Individual Artist Fellowship by a Minnesota Region Arts Council.

**Mary Koeberl** is a retired teacher, having taught high school, then elementary grades for over thirty-two years. She has had material published in the *Southeast Missourian* newspaper, *Good Old Days* and *Good Old Days Specials* magazine. She has had poetry accepted by *Country Woman* magazine and *Ideals* magazine. She is owner of a small business, M.K. Originals, which offers spiritual materials such as bookmarks, note cards, greeting cards, framed baptismal and wedding poems, and picture poems of area churches, all featuring her poetry. Mary Koeberl attends St. John's Evangelical Lutheran Church in Pocahontas, Missouri.

**Deb Kosmer** is the Bereavement Support Coordinator for Affinity Visiting Nurses Hospice. Ministry Homecare. Deb provides grief services to hospice patients, families and other grieving individuals in the Fox Valley in Wisconsin. Her services include grief group facilitation, individual counseling and grief education. She is a frequent speaker on the topic of grief in the community. She has a Master's degree in Social Work. Her grief poems and articles have been published in several grief publications including *Bereavement Magazine*, *The Compassionate Friends* national magazine, and *New Leaf Magazine*. Six of her poems have been reproduced as grief cards by New Leaf Resources.

**Connie Krueger** has thought in rhyme since she was very young, and has used that gift to fit most any person or situation that she found herself involved with over the years. Many pastors, choir members and directors, theater casts and crews, students her husband taught or coached, family, friends, fellow board members, and even strangers (if she could get enough "ammunition" from people who know them well) have found themselves in her poems. Her grandchildren have been receiving "Nonny cards" since they were born. That means more than 20 years for some of them. "There are many things that give me joy," she said, "but writing is definitely first on the list."

**Matthew R. Kruse** is currently completing his undergraduate degree in economics and religion at Augustana College in Sioux Falls, South Dakota. He plans to study to become an ordained minister within the Evangelical Lutheran Church in America (ELCA). He wrote "The Feeling of Silence" during the middle of a sixteen-hour-long vow of silence as a summer camp counselor.

**Mary Kuck** serves with her husband David as an ELCA Global Missions missionary, teaching communications skills at United Theological College in Kingston, Jamaica. She also teaches English part-time at HEART Trust/NTA, Jamaica's job training program. She has published poems in the *Connecticut River Review* (1978, 1983) and the *Hamden Chronicle* (1980). Other publications include *'Fi Mi' English Language Book* (Heart Trust/NTA 2004) and "Mi and Myself – Dual Identity in Jamaican English Language Speakers" in *Language Teacher Research in the Americas* (TESOL 2007). She and David have two children and two grandchildren, for whom she likes to make quilts.

**AnnJeanette Lee** was born and raised on a farm in Southern Minnesota. Animals were the main concern of hers as far as tending them and understanding their ways. Rather than doing dishes or house cleaning, she would tend the chickens and help her dad with chores and field work. Horses were her greatest love and soon she was able to ride, care for and drive them. She grew up on horseback on a 1918 army saddle, a Christmas present from Dad. AnnJeanette was baptized and confirmed in Lime Creek Lutheran Church on the state line of Minnesota and Iowa. Her schooling started in a one-room country school through eighth grade. She loved to read and write short stories and poems. Her passion for the written word is a continuous obsession. In 2002 she published her first book, *TALES OF TALES*.

**Elizabeth J. Leopard** was born in Colorado in 1929, and spent her early years in southern Illinois. She has composed poems and short stories for as long as she could write. She received little encouragement until Mickey Spillane saw some of her work and admonished her for not using her God given talent. She is retired from 20 years in Television and public radio. Due to physical restraints, she writes "when the mood strikes her."

**Nancy Lund** is originally from California, but transplanted her Lutheran roots from the Pacific Southwest to a more rural home overlooking the Mississippi River. Her enjoyments include all the bounty of small-town life, which offers many opportunities but rarely the option of being detached. She lives in Pepin, Wisconsin, with husband Fred and an assortment of small dogs.

**Lynda M. Maraby** and her family have been members of Salem Lutheran Church in Spokane, Washington for four generations. Baptized and confirmed in that congregation, she has recently returned to worship there after coming back to Spokane to teach English as a Second Language at Gonzaga University. She earned a BA in History and French from Whitworth College, a Licence ès Lettres in English and American literature from the Université de Paris (Sorbonne), and a Master of Arts in Romance Linguistics from the University of Washington. Her poetry publications include *Women's Uncommon Prayers* (Morehouse Press, 2000), *Lost and Found: Poetry on Buses 2003* (King County Department of Transportation), and a chapbook, *Sticks in Water*, 2004, under the auspices of the Seattle Writers' Association.

**David Melby-Gibbons** graduated in 2005 from St. Olaf College with a B.A. in Religion. Here he spent most of his time in the library but found time to meet and fall in love with his wife Christie. Recently married, they have since moved to Bethlehem, PA., where Christie is studying for her Master's of Divinity at Moravian Theological Seminary. David is employed as the part-time Director of Youth Ministry for Edgeboro Moravian Church where he also leads the music for their non-traditional worship service. David is also employed as a part-time cook and baker at Friends Café in Bethlehem. He spends the majority of his "free time" playing guitar, taking walks with Christie, reading, and occasionally writing poetry.

**Roberta Meyer** lives on a dairy farm in Southern Indiana with her husband and eighteen year old daughter. She also has two married children and four grandchildren. She is recently retiring from a thirty-three year career in elementary education and is entering the candidacy process for rostered ministry with the ELCA. Roberta is a commissioned lay worship leader for the I-K Synod of the ELCA. This gives her the opportunity to use her writing and speaking gifts in service to area churches. She also writes and gives children's sermons at her home congregation weekly. Besides writing Roberta enjoys drawing and painting, reading, swimming and hanging out with her two horses.

**Rebecca F. Miller** is currently finishing her Masters of Divinity at Luther Seminary. Her husband, Christopher, is also preparing for pastoral ministry.

**June L. Mita** has been writing poetry since she was 14. She began as a lyricist and composer, then settled on poetry. She has been a member of the Wit and Wisdom poetry club in Manchester, CT and she was also a member of the Connecticut Poetry Society from 1984 to 1990. It was at that point that she became a freelance journalist as well as an essayist. She gave up her writing in 1995 to raise her family. She is now picking up where she left off, starting once again with poetry and combining her pieces with another passion, photography. Her dream is to release a book of poetry with photos to bring the words alive visually.

**Elizabeth Musselman** is a Ph.D. student in theology at the University of Chicago Divinity School, a former hospital chaplain, and a candidate for ordained ministry in the ELCA. Her dissertation investigates the ways in which Martin Luther and Søren Kierkegaard's readings of Genesis 22 reveal their deepest convictions about what it means to live in faith before a God who is both revealed and hidden.

**Donna Beth Nelson** grew up in Portland, Oregon, and earned a BA in Education from Pacific Lutheran University. She lives in Seattle and is an active member of Bethany Lutheran Church. She enjoys poetry, art and music, and has been writing poetry for most of her life.

**Christie Nielsen** is an active member, including Altar Guild and Acolyte, of Ascension Lutheran Church in Boynton Beach, Florida. She has been happily married to Richard for 25 years and is a retired administrative assistant enjoying sunny south Florida after raising three sons in New York. Christie is now blessed with five delicious grandchildren. Her leisure passions are yoga, golf, cycling, and reading. Charities include the local food pantry, Lutheran Worldwide Hunger Relief, Pap Corp. for Cancer Research, The Humane Society of the United States, the ASPCA and swimming laps to raise money for The Red Cross International Relief Fund.

**Mark Patrick Odland** is a poet and visual artist from Alexandria, MN. A graduate of Augustana College and Luther Seminary, Mark currently serves as pastor of outreach and new ministry development at Living Waters Lutheran Church in Sauk Rapids, MN. Mark is happily married to Rachel, and they are expecting their first child (a little girl!) in September of 2007. Mark feels a strong calling to encourage, inspire, and nourish the arts within the larger church, and believes that the creation of *SIMUL – Lutheran Voices in Poetry*, is simply one of many ways to help make this a reality.

**Kirby Olson** studied poetry at Naropa Institute with Gregory Corso, Ed Dorn, Allen Ginsberg, and Ed Sanders. He is the author of *Comedy After Postmodernism, Andrei Codrescu & The Myth of America, Gregory Corso: Doubting Thomist, & Temping: A Novel*, and *Waiting for the Rapture*. He taught English and American Literature at a Finnish university for several years and is currently a professor of philosophy and literature at SUNY-Delhi. Kirby Olson is a member of the Immanuel Lutheran Church of Delhi, New York.

**Riitta Passananti** grew up in Finland along the shores of Lake Saimaa. From early childhood she had a deep sense of God's presence in all His creation and of His abiding grace. She is a member of Lutheran Church of the Good Shepherd. Her early years were lived close to the land on a small farm struggling with post-war shortages. She graduated from the University of Helsinki, and moved to Rhode Island after marrying her husband, but she travels home to Finland every summer, often accompanied by one of her three children. She has been writing poetry actively for two decades and has accumulated a large body of mostly unpublished work. She continues to write in English and her native Finnish.

**Nancy Payne**, a life-long resident of Illinois, escaped to Florida three years ago and luxuriates in the winter sunshine while empathizing with her old friends. Her work has appeared in *The Rockford Review*, *Koroné* and other "little literary" publications. A retired secretary, she delights in the time to write poetry and short stories.

**Edward Pease** is a member of Saint John's Evangelical Lutheran Church, "Church on the Hill," of Princeton, Illinois. He attended Wartburg College in Waverly, Iowa graduating Summa cum Laude with a major in Religion in 2006. He is attending Chandler School of Theology in Atlanta, Georgia in the Master's of Theological Studies Program. His work has been frequently published in *The Castle*, Wartburg College's literary magazine.

**Carlita L. Pedersen** was born, raised and educated in Iowa. She married in August 1940; the marriage lasted until her husband died in February 2000. She was a tag-along Army wife during World War II. Carlita lived in Omaha, Nebraska from July 1945 until October 2004. She has three children, nine grandchildren and twelve great grandchildren. She has had over 500 poems printed in various publications. Carlita has a life membership in the Nebraska Congress of Parents and Teachers and is a Past Matron of Eastern Star. She now lives in McKinney, Texas with her youngest son and his wife and attends Christ the Servant Lutheran Church in Allen, Texas. Carlita is 87 years old.

**Flo Pendergrast** is a retired Nurse Anesthetist with varied interests including gardening, church renewal, and society renewal. She has lived in Sweden, Mexico, on a Navajo reservation, and speaks Swedish and Spanish "pretty well." Flo has four grown children and one grandchild, is involved in the League of Women Voters, and is a member of a writing group which has published two books. She has also volunteered at Holden Village. Flo Pendergrast is a member of a small Spanish multicultural Lutheran church in Minnesota.

**Victor Harms Pera** arrived in Woodworth, ND on October 3rd, 1932 and in heaven April 1st, 2007. His father (born a Nestorian Christian in Persia) became a Lutheran Pastor in the U.S.A. and his mother was a German Lutheran from Russia. Victor was 5th of 13 Pera children, all of whom attended college, 5 becoming Lutheran Pastors and 4 Lutheran Church workers. He got his "parson's training" at Concordia, St. Paul and the St. Louis Seminary. He was Shepherd in Piper, Kansas, Sheboygan, Wisconsin, Newton, North Carolina and 30 years in Milwaukee, Wisconsin. Victor loved God, his wife of 50 years, his 3 children, his sheep, music, preaching, and writing poems to his wife and to Christ every Christmas.

**Marilyn Peretti** of Glen Ellyn, Illinois, created educational slide programs on four Central American countries and South Africa after she visited there in the late 1980s and early 1990s, to convey the inequities and oppression there. Her poetry has centered on nature and particularly elegant, endangered cranes. One of her self illustrated books is, *Let Wings Take You*. Her poems have been published in *Christian Science Monitor*, *Black Bear Review*, *California Quarterly*, *Seeding the Snow*, *Prairie Light Review*, and others. Her poetry has won awards from *Current* in Ann Arbor, The National Council on Aging, and The Labyrinth Society. She will be the featured artist of the Nature Artists Guild of The Morton Arboretum in November, 2007.

**Grant Perry** is a retired official reporter of debates, United States Senate. He retired from Federal service in 1979 and returned to Texas, where he has lived since. His first wife, Frances, died in 1983 and he married Joan (Joy) Hindman in 1985. As he would say, 3 daughters, 5 stepchildren, and 17 grandchildren "probably qualify him as a family man." Grant's poems have appeared in *Lucidity*, *The Wounded Heart*, *Poems by Iowa Elderhostelers 1988*, and several local poetry society anthologies. He is also the author of *Chicken Scratches – Grains of Truth*, an autobiographical volume printed for private distribution in 1991. Several of his essays have been published in *The Shorthand Reporter* and various Mensa publications.

**Jane Piirto** is Trustees' Professor at Ashland University in Ohio. She has been granted Individual Artist Fellowships in both poetry and in fiction from the Ohio Arts Council. She is a member of Trinity Lutheran Church, and is a Finnish-American. She is the author of 15 books and chapbooks, including the award-winning novel, *The Three-Week Trance Diet, A Location in the Upper Peninsula: Collected Poems, Stories, and Essays*, and *Journeys to Sacred Places*. She also writes on the psychology of creativity, and her book *My Teeming Brain: Understanding Creative Writers is a study of creativity in creative writers*. She is listed in the Directory of American Poets and Writers.

**Dorothea H. Pletta** wrote "With Love to Kevin" to honor the memory of her grandson who died in a car wreck on June 27, 1982 at the age of 17. He had just graduated from high school with honors. Some of his interests which are alluded to in the poem are: His car, a VW convertible which he had put a lot of time and energy into to refurbish; he was a drummer in the high school band; he played tennis on the high school tennis team; he worked at Wendy's and wore the required aqua and white striped shirt. He was 6'2" and had curly hair.

**Wayne L. Quam** is fifty-five years old and currently enrolled in his second year of seminary at the Lutheran Brethren Seminary in Fergus Falls, Minnesota. He has been a Lutheran all his life and was brought up in the ALC tradition in east central North Dakota. He has been married to Jacquie for thirty three years, who is his most ardent supporter. They have three children and seven grandchildren. About two years ago, God called him into the ministry, hence his current status as student in seminary. Two of Wayne's short stories and a poem have been published in *Plain Song*, a campus publication of Jamestown College.

**Ralph Quere** is a professor emeritus of history and theology at Wartburg Theological Seminary in Dubuque, Iowa. He and his wife of fifty years, Janice Meeter Quere, have had six children, three of whom are still living. Ralph studied at Princeton University, (served in the US Navy three years), Trinity Seminary, and Princeton Seminary for a PhD in historical theology. He served a rural parish in Iowa for three years. He taught (and teaches) Confessions and evangelism for over thirty years and visits their nine grandchildren in retirement. He says that he writes poetry "when he has to" in order to express emotions and ideas with which he is struggling.

**David Reiman** lives in Puyallup, Washington, and attends Pilgrim Lutheran Church. He is an eighth grader at Ferrucci Junior High, and is currently thirteen years of age. His passion is music, but began to write novels when he was about eleven because he enjoyed the creativity involved in it. He began writing lyrics when he was twelve because it went hand in hand with music. This led him to poetry because the music he listens to is mostly free-verse poetry.

**Lois Bertram Reiner** wrote "Later That Night..." as one of many "letters" to (the spirit of) her late husband, Walt "Schatz" Reiner, who died on Dec. 5, 2007. They had 54 years of an incredible life together. Whether these can be considered poems is the question. They formulate her literary approach to both healing and preserving certain memories. The invitation to submit work for *SIMUL – Lutheran Voices in Poetry* came via email right about the time she was participating in a Lutheran Women's writing workshop ("Growing Up Lutheran") in Chicago. So, she took heart. She had previous publications some years ago in *The Cresset*, Valparaiso University's magazine.

**Jessica Rivera** is a Lutheran Pastor in Minnesota. As both a Pastor and a Writer, Jessica regards those who write, sing and speak the stories and words of faith as modern versions of the ancient bard; speakers of the salvation story to all who listen. Jessica attributes her passion for the written word and its application in ministry to the deep faith and love of her family who surrounded her with love, faith, story and song.

**Theresa M. (Terry) Rochford** has been a member of Saint Peter's Lutheran Church in New York City for twelve years. She is currently working as an adjunct instructor for New York University in the Steinhardt School of Culture, Education and Human Development. Her interest in poetry began when she was in fifth grade and discovered the words of Robert Frost and Emily Dickinson. She says, "Poetry is the outlet for my struggle with life's contradictions."

**Mary Margaret Rode** is a retired teacher, having taught in the San Antonio School District for ten years and at St. Luke's Episcopal School for twenty-one years. She has a B.A. in English from Mary Hardin-Baylor University and an M.A. in Education from The University of Texas at San Antonio. Her only published poems were in the *San Antonio Express-News* "Book Page." She is a member of Christ Lutheran Church, Alamo Heights.

**Megan Rohrer** (The Rev.), a native of Sioux Falls, SD, graduated from Augustana College and went on to receive her master of divinity at the Pacific School of Religion in Berkeley, California. Megan has been called by a consortium of Lutheran Churches in San Francisco and appointed to the position of Director of The Welcome Ministry. Megan is also is heavily involved with several non-profit organizations including Pace e Bene, Good Soil, The Extraordinary Candidacy Project, the San Francisco Trans March and the Gender Pluralism Institute. Megan is a writer of curriculum, as well as an accomplished musician, artist, orator, and promoter and creator of internet activism for non-profit organizations.

**Sherry Knight Rossiter** is a lifelong Lutheran currently residing in Missoula, Montana, where she is an active member of St. Paul Lutheran Church. In the past, she has worked as an aviation flight and ground instructor, commercial airplane and helicopter pilot, an aviation journalist, a freelance writer, and an adjunct college professor. For the past seventeen years, she has been employed as a Licensed Clinical Professional Counselor in private practice. After a long hiatus, she is starting to do some freelance writing again. While she has been writing for over twenty-five years, she has only recently begun to write poetry. Sherry received Honorable Mention in the Non-rhyming Poem category of the 2001 Writer's Digest Writing Competition, which attracted around 19,000 entries.

**Janet Rowse** spent most of her adult life in Kennewick, Washington where she taught in the public schools. She also taught for over 20 years at the local community college, Columbia Basin College; in Pasco as an instructor in the Humanities Department. She taught writing, literature, and was in charge of the Learning Center. In 1992 she took an early retirement and eventually moved to North Dakota where the family farm is located. Janet and her son have had their farm verified as an organic farm. Janet is active in the local communities and volunteers as assistant pastor. She has had poems published in *The Journal*, and was first place winner in the North Dakota Mothers contest. She received Editor's Choice for Outstanding Achievement in Poetry from the *International Library of Poetry*.

**Peggy Rushton** is a poet and writer of short-story fiction. A member of Bergstrasse Lutheran Church, she lives in a converted barn in Lancaster County Pennsylvania along with her cat Simon. Peggy has studied as a writer at Rabbit Hill Writers' Studio, and most recently completed three creative writing courses in poetry at Emerson college, Sussex England. Publications include a short story published in *Phase Magazine*, a small literary magazine that features new Pennsylvania writers; poetry in *Peering Crystalline*, the literary magazine printed by Emerson college, Sussex England; 2 poems published in the local Lutheran Church Magazine, *The Bell*; and a poem accepted to be published in an upcoming book, *Standing on Words*, by poet-author Paul Mathews, and published by Hawthorn Press. This is to be released in June of this year.

**Andy Rutrough** has been a pastor for fifteen years, four of them in South Williamsport, PA and eleven at St. Thomas Lutheran Church in Richmond, Kentucky where he currently serves. He has published a poem in *Lutheran Partners*, and in 2005 wrote a story a week for *Being Human* radio, a half hour radio show in Mt. Vernon, Washington. He is currently working on his first book, *Happy Hour* *and Other Stories*. He grew up in coastal Mississippi, took a BA in English, religion and Latin at St. Olaf College, an MA in English at University of Virginia, and Master of Divinity at LSTC. Currently he lives in Curtis Pike Community; a prayer based Christian intentional community that emphasizes environmental sustainability, social justice, and work for peace.

**Winnie Sawrun** has always loved the written word, but only recently gave into publishing poetry which is of a very personal nature. She writes about current events and moral issues. Her recent poems have been published in several volumes and on tape and CD. The publications include *America at the Millennium, Best Poets of 2000*, and the *Sound of Poetry*. Winnie says all good poetry should be read aloud.

**Suzanne S. Schaffer** is a life-long Lutheran and a member at Grace Lutheran Church, Hubbard, OH. With both bachelor and master degrees in education, she has taught all age groups, and focused mainly on reading and literacy. Now retired, she volunteers at the local elementary school and for WOW, an after school program for under privileged youngsters. She serves on the Northeastern Ohio Synod Council and is a board member and volunteer at the Trumbull Art Gallery. She and her husband, a Lutheran pastor, are the parents of three and grandparents of four. The birth of their first granddaughter prompted a submission of a piece, "Balance," to Walter Wangerin's *Lutheran Vespers* which he used on a broadcast in 1999.

**Jerry L. Schmalenberger** is the retired President of Pacific Lutheran Theological Seminary, Berkeley, California. Since retirement he has been serving as an ELCA Global Mission Volunteer in South America, Jamaica, Germany, Myanmar, Liberia West Africa, Sumatra Indonesia and Hong Kong. Many of his poems are set in those cultures. He has published one book of poems which he often reads at a local coffee house titled *In Celebration*. He has authored 22 books on Practical Theology. A few of his poems have appeared in *A Celebration of Poets, Ruah, Best Poems of 1998*, and *Best Poems of the 90s*.

**Diane Scholl** is Professor of English at Luther College, Decorah, Iowa, where she has taught since 1978. She earned her B.A. in English from St. Olaf College in 1968, her M.A. (1969) and Ph.D. (1973) from The University of Chicago. Her interests include American literature, English and American poetry, particularly of the seventeenth century and modern periods, women's literature, and theology and literature. She has published essays on Emily Dickinson, Nathaniel Hawthorne, Robert Lowell and Alice Walker, and poetry in *The Cresset* and *College English*. Recent projects include a reading list and book discussions on campus of texts that link science and humanities, designed to inspire interdisciplinary teaching, and research on American "Orientalism" and nineteenth-century women's literature. Favorite poets include George Herbert, John Donne, Emily Dickinson and Seamus Heaney.

**Elise Seyfried** is Director of Spiritual Formation at Christ's Lutheran Church in Oreland, PA. She is also a playwright, essayist and award-winning lyricist (Stanley Drama Award for *Flight*, a musical about Howard Hughes). Her works have appeared in such diverse publications as *Guideposts* and the *Wittenburg Door*. Elise is living with bipolar disorder, and finds the Lutheran theology of grace a great comfort.

**Paul Shepherd** is the winner of the Mary McCarthy Prize in Fiction. His novel, *More like Not Running Away*, was published in January 2006 by Sarabande Books. He was also a finalist for the AWP Award in the novel, for the James Jones, and for the Breadloaf/Bakeless. His work has appeared in *Prairie Schooner, Margie, William and Mary Review, Pacific Review, Folio*, and other journals. He's served as Senior Editor at *International Quarterly*. He is Writer-in-Residence and a former Kingsbury Fellow at Florida State University.

**Donna Simmons** is a graduate of the University of New Hampshire and McIntosh College. She is a semi-retired accountant, educator, and writer, and an active member of Holy Cross Lutheran Church in Kennebunk, Maine where she sings in the choir, occasionally co-facilitates a grief and loss group, and teaches creative writing to willing friends during summer break. Donna writes poetry and short stories. She has published a memoir: *A Fork in the Road: My Story of Suicide and Survival* [Trafford, 2005] and contributed a collection of short pieces and poetry to an anthology: *Mainely Driftwood* [Trafford, 2004]. She lives with her husband, Bill, in the forest on the edge of the rural community of Alfred, Maine.

**Gregory Holmes Singleton** was born in Florence, Alabama, in 1940. After almost four decades of university teaching he retired in 2005. Singleton is Professor of History, Emeritus, at Northeastern Illinois University, and is the author of many publications, including *Religion in the City of Angels: American Protestant Culture and Urbanization, Los Angeles 1850-1930* (Ann Arbor: UMI Research Press, 1979). He is on the Editorial Council of *Let's Talk: Living Theology in the Metropolitan Chicago Synod* (Evangelical Lutheran Church in America). Singleton lives in Chicago, Illinois, with his wife, Jeannine, and their cat/owner, Zane.

**Jerry Smith** became interested in poetry during high school and this interest blossomed in college, where he majored in English. He has worked as an apprentice draftsman, a U.S. Government employee, a teacher from middle school to graduate level and as an administrator. He also studied for the Lutheran ministry. He has written poetry seriously since 1996, has published poems in several magazines and anthologies, and has won awards in state and national contests. One of his poems, "The Smiles," was set to music by writer Lee Chapman and sung locally by baritone Howard Swyers. He has read his poems in a variety of settings and taught poetry units in high school classes. He is married, has two children and four grandchildren.

**Ren Snyder** was born in Kentucky in 1950, and grew up in Ann Arbor, the eldest son of a middle school Science teacher and a high school English teacher. He fell in love with Susan Martin in 1968, following (stalking) her to church and weekend youth activities. Married to Susan since 1970, they have two (now adult) children, Carrie and Todd, and are expectant grandparents. Ren is active in Trinity Lutheran Church, and is a writer, performer, teacher, student, guitar player, singer, runner, and beer drinker (in the Martin Luther tradition). He claims to be addicted to word play and expression and that his greatest conceit is attempting to make sense of seemingly improbable ideas.

**Cathryn A. Spelts** is a retired college professor (SDSM&T). After selling her home last year, she is adjusting to apartment living sans a flower garden. She is active in a Bible study, Book Club, and her church, South Canyon Lutheran. She plays golf, bridge, and Mah Jongg.

**Dick Stahl** taught English at Davenport Central High School for 34 and a half years, retiring in 2001. His fascination with the Mississippi River fires his poems. He and his wife, Helen, are members of St. Paul Lutheran Church in Davenport, Iowa. He graduated from Augustana College (B.A.) in 1963, from the University of Iowa (M.A.) in 1970, and from Western Illinois University (Ed.S.) in 1981. His three books of poetry include *After the Milk Route* (1988), *Under the Green Tree Hotel* (1996), and *Mr. Farnam's Guests* (2004). His poems have appeared in *Saga, English Journal, Farmer's Market, River Oak Review, Voices on the Landscape: Contemporary Iowa Poets, Lyrical Iowa, Big Muddy*, and *Buffalo Carp*.

**Kimberly Stenerson** has been writing for over twenty years and has received an MA in Creative Writing from Western Illinois University. She currently lives on a farm outside of Barneveld with her husband Kirk and two children, Adam and Jillian. She credits her love of poetry and storytelling on having been exposed at an early age to the lyric and stories found in the Bible.

**Doris Stengel** grew up in North Dakota but has been a resident of Minnesota for 45 years. She teaches part time at the Brainerd Area Education Center and mentors students in poetry from elementary age to teenage. Doris is a member of Heartland Poets, League of Minnesota Poets and President of the National Poetry Society. The past five years she has chaired the national Stevens Manuscript Competition. She has previously been published in: *Dust & Fire,*

*Lakes Country Journal, Paper Moon, Encore, North Dakota Horizons, Her Voice.*

**Roberta C. Stewart** first was "invited to be a poet" by college room-mates while at Northwestern University during the 1960's. There, she studied writing through the School of Journalism and earned her degree in political science. Poetry became an important life tool for spiritual growth. She continues to develop her craft in classes, workshops, and writing groups, and has received acclaim for skilled editing from poets Molly Peacock and Ellen Kort. Roberta was selected first Poetry Editor of the *Fox Valley Arts Beat Magazine.* Her poems have appeared in various journals, including *Prairie Light Review, Batavia Writers' Workshop Annual, Kane County Chronicle,* and *Fox Valley Arts Beat Magazine.* She currently is a student with The Innermission School of Spiritual Companioning.

**Charles Strietelmeier** is pastor of Augustana Lutheran Church in Hobart, Indiana. He has previously published poems in the *Cresset* magazine, and in *Lutheran Partners.*

**Verna Summerville** believes that her gift is one to be shared with family and friends, so that's what she does with most of her writings. She grew up in Indiana and came to Wisconsin as a new bride. Still married to her loving husband of 46 years, she is now a mom, granny, and great-grandma. Her interests are poetry, crochet, cross-stitch, and oil painting. She also enjoys her volunteer hours at church. Verna has previously published poetry and a short story in *The Lutheran Journal.*

**Steve Swanson** has taught at five Lutheran colleges and the University of Oregon, and has served as Director of Creative Writing for two of these colleges. A graduate of Luther Seminary, in addition to his teaching responsibilities Steve has served 40 congregations, primarily as an interim pastor. In the '70s he was Poetry Editor of the *Lutheran Standard.* Currently, Steve Swanson teaches Creative Writing at Waldorf College.

**Fran Swarbrick** is married to a retired Lutheran pastor, is a former newspaper reporter and is currently a museum curator. She is also an artist specializing in rural and historic scenes. She and her husband have lived in the Illinois towns of Anna, Pekin, Carthage, and now reside in rural Dixon. Fran Swarbrick's articles and poems have been published in *Cappers*, *Frontiers*, *Ladies' Home Journal*, *The Lutheran*, *The Lutheran Quarterly*, *Midstream*, *Mature Years*, *Outdoor Illinois*, *Angels on Earth*, and *Passenger Magazine*.

**Melanie J. Taormina** is a life-long Lutheran and a member of St. Luke Lutheran Church in Williamsport, PA. She holds a MFA in writing from the University of Pittsburgh and works for her under-graduate alma mater, Lycoming College, as Director of Alumni Relations. Her poems have appeared in the *Pittsburg Post-Gazette* and *Time of Singing*. She lives with her husband of eleven years, Dan, and their cat Tabby, and seeks to embrace the joys large and small each of life's days.

**Diane Tremper** always has a pen and paper to scribble notes, thoughts, and often a poem. She received her BA in education from Trenton State College and her MA in reading specialization from Kean University. Her teaching experiences have ranged from infants to seniors, in day care, public schools, private schools, and work-shops. Sandwiched in there was an assignment as parish worker to St. John's Lutheran Church, Newark, NJ, where she found a home in the LCA. She remains an active member there and currently works part time at the Maplewood Library. She enjoys music and biking, where thoughts percolate.

**Sandee Gertz Umbach** lives and writes in Washington, Pennsylvania where she is an active member of First Lutheran Church. She received a Pennsylvania Council on the Arts fellowship in poetry in 2000 and won the 1999 Sandburg-Livesay Award for her winning poem, "I Can't Help But Think About Eve" published in the anthology *No Choice But To Trust*, by Mekler Deahl of Hamilton, Canada. Her work has appeared in many literary journals and anthologies, including *The Pittsburg Quarterly*, *The Potomac Review*, *The Ledge*,

*Poet Lore, Sistersong: Women Across Cultures, Taproot Literary Journal*, and in the Spring 2007 Edition of *poetrymagazine.com*. Her manuscript has taken Honorable Mention in the Acorn Rukeyser Chapbook Award competition, published by Mekler and Deahl. She founded and operates a non-profit arts center devoted to low-income children.

**Arlet Vollers** began her writing career early in life but serious efforts to publish date from the late 1970's when she retired from teaching. Since then her work in non-fiction, several devotional series, and poetry has appeared in numerous denominational and secular publications for both children and adults. In recent years poetry has been her forte and she has won numerous poetry awards. She is a charter member of Sacramento Christian Writers and has membership in California Writer's Club, California Federation of Chaparral Poets, several local writing groups, and until recently the Society of Children's Book Writers and Illustrators.

**Frank A. Vollmer**, husband, parent, grandparent, great grandparent, poet, retired, he is 80 years young with a deeply religious bent but more to the liberal side. He was recently on staff of Camp Calumet in New Hampshire (A Lutheran camp and conference center). He now is active in Thrivent and St. Andrew in Atlantic City. He has continual interest in social justice issues. He is a cancer and stroke survivor.

**Hannah Wallisch** has been involved in the Lutheran church through both her home congregation and through the ELCA's Board of the Lutheran Youth Organization, on which she served a three-year term as a regional member-at-large. She has spent the past three summers as a counselor and program assistant at a Lutheran summer camp in Wisconsin, where she got to play outside all day, garden, go camping, build fires, and talk about God with campers – paradise, you might say (and so does she). She is currently completing her senior year as a student at St. Olaf College in Northfield, MN, where she majors in English and Women's Studies and scribbles poems whenever she gets a chance to.

**Kate Walters** is a previously unpublished poet who is currently working as a Peace Corps Volunteer in Jordan, in the Middle East. Her responsibilities include teaching fifth and sixth grade English and remedial classes. Before moving to Jordan, she attended Appalachian State University and received a Bachelor's Degree in Interdisciplinary Studies. Her family lives in Tennessee and includes her mother, father, sister, and a dog.

**David Webb** graduated from the Ohio State University in 2005 with a degree in English and Creative Writing of Poetry. His work has been published in the University of Cincinnati's *Short Vine*. Currently David is the youth director, catechism teacher, and lay worship assistant at Calvary Lutheran Church in Chillicothe, Ohio. He hopes to begin his diaconal training at Trinity Lutheran Seminary next fall studying Christian Spirituality and Formation. In the mean-while he is teaching himself to play the guitar, listening to T.K. Webb (no relation) and reading his favorite poet Kevin Young to his Pekinese beagle mix, General Cornwallis.

**Roy B. Wingate** graduated from Central Seminary in Fremont, Nebraska, and was pastor at Resurrection Lutheran Church in Ames, Nebraska, and St. John's Lutheran Church in Schuyler, Nebraska, before moving to Iowa City, Iowa. He served as pastor at Gloria Dei Lutheran Church for thirty six years in Iowa City.

**Ellen Roberts Young** published her first chapbook, *Accidents*, through Finishing Line Press in 2004. She has poems anthologized in *Orpheus and Company* (Deborah DeNicola, editor) and *The Wisdom of Daughters* (R.H. Finger and K. Sandhaas, editors) as well as publications in numerous journals. She works as a copy-editor and researcher. She recently moved from Pennsylvania to Las Cruces, New Mexico. Ellen Roberts Young has over 100 publications including *Alive Now*, *Christian Century*, *Earth's Daughters*, *Embers*, *Evansville Review*, *Into the Teeth of the Wind*, *The Kerf*, *The Other Side*, *Rockhurst Review*, and *Slant*.

**Marion H. Youngquist** was a reporter/feature writer for several newspapers, and for a decade contributed to *The Lutheran* and edited church publications for Wisconsin/Upper Michigan. She is a prize-winning poet, and has had her work included in a twelve-song cycle by composer Cheryl Zehfus. She belongs to many poetry organizations, and has written two prize-winning plays. Her historical novel *Procula* was published in 2005; *Maple Tree Tales* (interrelated short stories) in 2006; *Christmas Presence*, a poetry book, will be released this fall. She and her husband Ted, a retired Lutheran Minister, have four children, six grandchildren and four great-granddaughters. The Youngquists live in Wauwatosa, WI.

**Jennifer Zarth** has a degree in English Literature from the University of Minnesota and works as a fundraising consultant for Community Health Charities Minnesota. She lives with her husband, a Lutheran pastor, and their children in Richfield, Minnesota. Jennifer Zarth's poems have appeared in the *1999 Minnesota Calendar*, *Minnesota Monthly*, *Sidewalks*, *North Coast Review*, *Re-Imagining Quarterly* and *Loonfeather*.

Printed in the United States
87848LV00005B/157-348/A